# Angels, Demons and the Armour of God

Andrew J. Lamont-Turner

Published by Andrew J. Lamont-Turner, 2024.

ANGELS, DEMONS AND THE ARMOUR OF GOD

**First edition. April 4, 2024.**



ISBN: 979-8224438389

Written by Andrew J. Lamont-Turner.

# Angels, Demons and the Armour of God
## The Unseen Struggle



---

Scripture quotations marked CSB have been taken from the Christian Standard Bible®, Copyright © 2017 by Holman Bible Publishers. Used by permission. Christian Standard Bible® and CSB® are federally registered trademarks of Holman Bible Publishers.

Scripture quotations marked WEB have been taken from the World English Bible. Public Domain.

The author uses Google Translate to translate this manuscript into other languages besides English.

---

Cover Page Design By AJ Lamont-Turner
Picture by Lancios2[1] or Pixabay

---

# Foreword

As I began writing this book, I grappled with a profound dilemma: how does one explore the depths of evil while remaining grounded in a personal faith? This tension between exploring the darker aspects of spiritual warfare and maintaining a steadfast commitment to God proved challenging and illuminating.

In these pages, you will thoroughly examine evil: its origins, manifestations throughout history, and relentless assaults on humanity. From the temptations faced by our earliest ancestors to the persecution of believers in the end times, the narrative of spiritual warfare unfolds with stark clarity. We confront the sobering reality of spiritual deception, corruption, and oppression that permeate our world.

Yet, amidst the darkness, there is a counterbalance—a beacon of hope that shines brightly against evil. Throughout this exploration, I have sought to emphasise the understanding of God: His sovereignty, goodness, and unwavering presence amid spiritual warfare. For every account of spiritual attack, there is a testimony of divine protection. For every instance of deception, there is a revelation of truth.

Indeed, this book is not merely a chronicle of evil but a celebration of faith—a testament to the transformative power of a strong and unwavering belief in God. As believers battle against the spiritual forces of darkness, they do not stand alone. They are fortified by the promises of Scripture, emboldened by the indwelling presence of the Holy Spirit, and empowered by the victorious work of Jesus Christ.

While writing these pages, I have been reminded of the importance of maintaining a personal faith that anchors us in life's storms, sustains us in times of trial, and empowers us to stand firm against the schemes of the enemy. I hope this book explores evil and is a source of inspiration and encouragement for believers engaged in spiritual warfare.

May you be strengthened in your faith as you journey through these pages. May you be equipped with the knowledge and discernment necessary to recognise and resist the forces of darkness. May you be filled with hope and assurance, knowing that the victory has already been won through our Lord and Savior, Jesus Christ.

Blessings,

Andrew

# Introduction

# Purpose of the Book

In spiritual understanding, the dichotomy of good and evil has been a central theme throughout human history. The eternal struggle between the forces of light and darkness played out in the biblical narratives has been a source of fascination and intrigue for believers and non-believers alike. In this book, "Angels, Demons, and the Armour of God: The Unseen Struggle," we journey through the pages of the Christian Bible to explore the profound and mysterious entities known as angels and demons.

## Biblical Foundations

THE PRIMARY PURPOSE of this book is to provide a comprehensive exploration of angels and demons from the Christian Bible perspective. We begin by establishing a solid biblical foundation for our understanding. The Bible is our authoritative source, containing numerous references to these celestial and infernal beings.

Angels and demons appear throughout the Old and New Testaments, often playing critical roles in God's divine plan. The first mention of angels in the Bible comes in the book of Genesis, where they are messengers of God, performing various tasks such as delivering divine messages, protecting individuals, and even delivering judgments (Genesis 16:7-14; Genesis 19:1-16). In the New Testament, angels are pivotal figures in the events surrounding the birth of Jesus, heralding the Good News to shepherds (Luke 2:8-15) and ministering to Christ during His temptation in the wilderness (Matthew 4:11).

On the opposing side of the spectrum, demons or unclean spirits also find their place in the Bible. They are depicted as malevolent entities, often associated with illness, affliction, and possession. One prominent example is the encounter between Jesus and a man possessed by demons in the region of the Gadarenes (Mark 5:1-20).

The Bible repeatedly demonstrates the reality of demonic forces and their interactions with humanity.

## Warning Against Angelolatry

THIS BOOK'S SIGNIFICANT emphasis is addressing the dangers associated with the veneration of angels, known as angelolatry. The Christian Bible explicitly commands believers to worship God alone. In the Old Testament, we find this directive in the Ten Commandments: "You shall have no other gods before me" (Exodus 20:3). The New Testament reaffirms this principle when Jesus declares, "You shall worship the Lord your God, and him only shall you serve" (Matthew 4:10).

However, as the pages of history have shown, the veneration of angels has sometimes overshadowed the worship of the one true God. This book draws attention to this error and highlights the importance of devotion exclusively to God. Angelolatry, though often well-intentioned, diverts the believer's focus from the Creator to the created beings. We aim to provide readers with a biblical understanding of angelic roles and their purpose as God's messengers and servants, not objects of worship.

## The Unseen War: Angels and Demons

ANOTHER CRITICAL OBJECTIVE is unveiling the unseen war between angels and demons. While these spiritual battles are often hidden from our physical senses, the Christian Bible provides glimpses into this cosmic struggle. The apostle Paul, in his letter to the Ephesians, vividly describes this conflict: "For we do not wrestle against flesh and blood, but against the rulers, against the authorities, against the cosmic powers over this present darkness, against the spiritual forces of evil in the heavenly places" (Ephesians 6:12).

This passage in Ephesians serves as the foundation for our exploration of the spiritual warfare that impacts the lives of believers.

By understanding the dynamics of this unseen battle, readers can better appreciate the challenges and trials they face in their spiritual journey. We explore the consequences for believers when they become unwitting participants in this celestial conflict and how to guard against negative spiritual influences.

## Equipping with the Armor of God

LASTLY, THIS BOOK EMPHASISES the vital role of the "Armor of God" in the believer's life. The apostle Paul, in the same Ephesians passage, outlines this spiritual armour, which includes the "belt of truth," "breastplate of righteousness," "shoes of the gospel of peace," "shield of faith," "helmet of salvation," and "sword of the Spirit" (Ephesians 6:14-17). These elements are essential for a Christian to stand firm in spiritual adversity.

We explore how each piece of armour serves as a defensive or offensive tool against the tactics of the devil and his demons. Understanding the significance of the armour empowers believers to protect themselves from spiritual oppression and actively engage in the spiritual battle.

## Practical Applications

AS WE JOURNEY THROUGH this book, readers will not only gain an enriched biblical understanding of angels, demons, and the spiritual battle but also practical applications for their daily lives. We provide guidance on how to recognise angelic and demonic influences, exercise spiritual discernment, and utilise the armour of God for spiritual warfare. Our goal is to equip believers with the knowledge and tools to navigate the unseen struggle, protect their faith, and remain steadfast in their devotion to God.

In the following pages, we will explore the biblical narratives more deeply, exploring the appearances and roles of angels and demons. We will also examine real-life applications of these spiritual truths, helping readers to walk in the light, even in the unseen struggle. May you be enlightened, encouraged, and equipped to stand firm in your faith and devotion to the one true God as we journey together.

Before we explore deeper into the world of angels and demons as portrayed in the Christian Bible, it's essential to set the stage by understanding the broader context in which these supernatural entities exist. Though often hidden from our physical senses, the spiritual realm plays a profound role in the biblical narrative and the lives of believers.

## The Spiritual Realm in the Bible

THE CHRISTIAN BIBLE introduces us to a universe beyond the physical world. It reveals the existence of a spiritual dimension inhabited by both heavenly and malevolent beings. The Bible's pages open with the creation account, describing God's work in shaping the heavens and the earth. This narrative lays the foundation for understanding the physical world and alludes to the presence of spiritual beings.

In the book of Genesis, we find that God created the heavens and the earth (Genesis 1:1). This broad term, "heavens," encompasses the physical and spiritual realms. The Bible's references to the "heavenly places" and the "heavenly realms" allude to this spiritual dimension. For example, the apostle Paul writes to the Ephesians, "In the heavenly places" (Ephesians 1:3), indicating that there is more to existence than what we perceive with our senses.

The spiritual realm is portrayed as a realm of order and hierarchy. The Bible introduces us to heavenly hosts, angels, archangels, and seraphim, each with distinct roles and responsibilities. These celestial beings are portrayed as messengers, servants, and worshipers of God. The prophet Isaiah's vision provides a glimpse into this heavenly hierarchy, as he witnessed seraphim in the presence of God, crying out, "Holy, holy, holy is the Lord of hosts" (Isaiah 6:1-3).

Conversely, the spiritual realm also contains malevolent entities, chief among them being Satan and the demons. Satan, formerly an angel, rebelled against God, and this rebellion is depicted in the Bible. In the book of Isaiah, we find a description of Lucifer's fall: "You said in your heart, 'I will ascend to heaven; above the stars of God I will set my throne on high'" (Isaiah 14:13). This fall marked the beginning of the spiritual conflict in the heavenly realms.

## The Cosmic Battle

THE EXISTENCE OF THIS cosmic battle, often referred to as the angelic rebellion or the war in heaven, sets the stage for the ongoing spiritual struggle between angels and demons. This conflict is not confined to the spiritual realm alone; it has far-reaching consequences for humanity.

The book of Revelation provides significant insights into this cosmic battle. In Revelation 12, the apostle John describes a vision of a woman, a dragon, and a war in heaven. The woman symbolises the people of God, and the dragon represents Satan, who seeks to destroy God's plan. In this heavenly war, we see Michael and his angels fighting against the dragon and his angels (Revelation 12:7). This imagery demonstrates that the conflict between good and evil is not isolated to the physical world but extends into the spiritual realms.

The consequences of this cosmic battle reverberate throughout human history. The fall of Satan and the presence of demonic forces introduce evil and suffering into the world. The Book of Job vividly illustrates how spiritual battles can impact human lives. Job, a righteous man, becomes the target of Satan's attacks, leading to immense suffering and trials. The dialogues between Job and his friends reflect the perplexing question of human suffering in the face of spiritual warfare.

From the inception of God's divine plan for the Messiah, a relentless adversary has worked tirelessly to thwart it. The Devil, in his malevolent cunning, has sought to derail the redemptive purpose of

God from the Garden of Eden to the Cross of Calvary. In this chapter, we explore the instances where Satan actively attempted to disrupt God's plan for the Messiah, examining his crafty strategies to hinder the promised deliverance.

**The Deception in the Garden of Eden:** The treacherous journey of the Devil's derailment begins in the Garden of Eden. God created a paradise where Adam and Eve lived perfectly with Him. However, Satan, disguised as a serpent, entered this idyllic setting with a sinister agenda. He cast doubt on God's command, insinuating that partaking of the forbidden fruit would elevate Adam and Eve to divine knowledge. This deception sowed the seeds of disobedience, leading to the first sin (Genesis 3:1-7).

This transgression introduced sin into the world, breaking the harmony between humanity and God. The enmity between the offspring of the woman and the serpent, as prophesied in Genesis 3:15, foreshadowed the spiritual battle that would ensue.

**The Corruption of Humanity:** Satan's next strategy involved corrupting humanity. The Devil's influence became increasingly apparent in the generations that followed Adam and Eve. He enticed humanity into wickedness, leading to a world filled with violence and depravity (Genesis 6:5-13). In this era, the righteous Noah and his family were chosen for salvation through the ark, ensuring the survival of God's plan (Genesis 7:1).

**The Tower of Babel and the Dispersal of Humanity:** After the Great Flood, humanity united again in opposition to God's plan. At the Tower of Babel, people sought to build a tower to reach the heavens, attempting to usurp God's authority (Genesis 11:1-9). God confused their language in response, causing them to scatter across the earth. This dispersion served to prevent a united rebellion against His purpose.

**The Israelites' Bondage in Egypt:** As the time for the Messiah's arrival drew nearer, the Devil's attacks intensified. The Israelites, the chosen people through whom the Messiah would come, were enslaved in Egypt for centuries. Pharaoh's oppressive regime aimed to annihilate them, but God's miraculous deliverance through Moses prevailed (Exodus 3:7-10, Exodus 12:31-42).

**The Attacks on the Lineage of the Messiah:** Throughout the Old Testament, Satan launched relentless attacks on the lineage through which the Messiah would be born. He targeted Tamar (Genesis 38), Rahab (Joshua 2:1-21), Ruth (Ruth 3:1-9), and Bathsheba (2 Samuel 11), but God's providence preserved the Messianic line.

**The Temptation of Jesus in the Wilderness:** As the prophesied Messiah, Jesus was the primary target of Satan's schemes. In the wilderness, Satan attempted to tempt Jesus into forsaking His divine mission. He questioned Jesus' identity, tempted Him with power, and suggested that He worshipped Satan (Matthew 4:1-11). Yet, Jesus remained unwavering, defeating Satan with the Word of God.

**The Plot to Kill the Messiah:** Satan's ultimate attempt to derail God's plan was the crucifixion of Jesus. He influenced the religious leaders of the day to conspire against Jesus and have Him crucified. Little did Satan know that this very crucifixion would be the means of his ultimate defeat. The Cross, which appeared to be Satan's victory, became humanity's salvation.

Throughout the ages, Satan tirelessly sought to derail God's plan for the Messiah. Still, divine providence, key individuals' faithfulness, and Christ's redemptive power prevailed. The Messiah's arrival and sacrifice at Calvary secured humanity's salvation, proving that even the darkest adversarial intentions cannot thwart God's sovereign will.

## The Role of Angels and Demons in Human Affairs

THE CHRISTIAN BIBLE reveals that angels and demons play significant roles in human affairs. The book of Daniel showcases angelic intervention in response to the prayers of a devout man. When

Daniel sought understanding through prayer and fasting, an angel was dispatched to provide insights and revelations (Daniel 9:20-23).

Conversely, demons are portrayed as malevolent entities seeking to influence and oppress humanity. The New Testament is replete with instances of demon possession and the suffering it brings. In Mark 5, we encounter the story of a man possessed by a legion of demons who tormented him. This narrative not only demonstrates the destructive power of demonic influence but also the authority of Jesus to cast out these evil spirits (Mark 5:1-20).

The role of angels and demons in human affairs is not limited to the pages of the Bible but extends into contemporary theological beliefs. For many believers, the concept of guardian angels offers comfort and assurance of divine protection. These guardian angels are seen as messengers and protectors assigned to watch over and guide individuals. While this belief is not explicitly detailed in the Bible, it is deeply rooted in Christian tradition.

On the opposite side of the spectrum, exorcism and spiritual warfare have become prominent themes in modern Christianity. The belief in the need for spiritual cleansing and deliverance from demonic influences has sparked the growth of specialised ministries and practices aimed at combating the forces of darkness.

## The Relevance for Believers

UNDERSTANDING THE SPIRITUAL realm and the roles of angels and demons is not merely an academic pursuit but holds significant relevance for believers. The Bible repeatedly emphasises the need for spiritual discernment and vigilance. The apostle Peter cautions, "Be sober-minded; be watchful. Your adversary, the devil, prowls around like a roaring lion, seeking someone to devour" (1 Peter 5:8). This warning emphasises the very real presence of spiritual adversaries and the necessity of equipping oneself for the battle.

Recognising the existence of the spiritual realm and the cosmic battle emphasises the importance of faith and spiritual fortitude. In his discussion of the Armor of God, the apostle Paul emphasises the need for believers to "stand firm" in the face of spiritual attacks (Ephesians 6:13). This spiritual armour protects against the schemes of the devil and his demons.

By setting the stage for understanding the spiritual realm, we pave the way for a deeper exploration of angels, demons, and the armour of God in the subsequent chapters. The cosmic battle between good and evil, played out in heavenly and earthly realms, forms the backdrop against which the believer's faith and spiritual journey unfolds. The Christian Bible provides the rich tapestry within which we will continue to unravel the profound truths about these celestial and malevolent entities and the ongoing unseen struggle.

## Angel Appearances, Christophanies, and Theophanies

IN THE VAST TAPESTRY of biblical narratives, encounters with heavenly beings, divine manifestations, and direct revelations from God are not uncommon. These encounters can be fascinating, but they also demand a nuanced understanding to discern between them. This section will explore the differences between angel appearances, Christophanies, and Theophanies.

### 1. Angel Appearances

Angelic appearances in the Bible are perhaps the most common type of divine encounter. As messengers of God, angels serve various roles, from delivering important messages to providing guidance, protection, and even supernatural interventions. While angelic appearances can be awe-inspiring, they are distinct from Christophanies and Theophanies.

Angels typically appear as messengers sent by God to interact with humans. Their appearances are marked by their angelic nature, and they often bring messages or instructions from God. Examples of angelic appearances are numerous in the Bible, such as the angel Gabriel appearing to the Virgin Mary to announce the birth of Jesus (Luke 1:26-38) or the angel who appeared to the shepherds to proclaim the birth of Christ (Luke 2:8-14).

## 2. Christophanies

Christophonies refer to the appearances of Jesus Christ in the Old Testament before His incarnation as a human being. These appearances are essential for understanding the unity of the Old and New Testaments and the preexistence of Christ. They provide a glimpse into the divine nature of Jesus.

One well-known Christophony is the encounter between Abraham and the "Angel of the Lord" in Genesis 18. In this narrative, the Angel of the Lord also referred to as the Lord Himself, appeared to Abraham. Through this encounter, the promise of Isaac's birth was reaffirmed. Many scholars believe this "Angel of the Lord" was a Christophony, a pre-incarnate appearance of Jesus.

Another notable Christophony occurs in the burning bush encounter with Moses. When God appeared to Moses in the burning bush, the text identifies God as the speaker (Exodus 3:4). However, in Stephen's speech in Acts 7:30-35, this being is referred to as the "Angel" who spoke to Moses on Mount Sinai, which suggests a Christophony.

## 3. Theophanies

Theophanies are direct manifestations of God's presence or His glory. They often involve awe-inspiring and overwhelming experiences that reveal the majesty and holiness of God. Theophanies serve to emphasise God's transcendence and His direct interaction with humanity.

One of the most famous Theophanies is the burning bush encounter mentioned earlier, where God revealed His presence to Moses. Another notable Theophany is when God appeared on Mount Sinai to give the Ten Commandments to the Israelites. The mountain was enveloped in smoke, fire, and thunder, displaying God's divine glory and holiness (Exodus 19:16-20).

It's important to differentiate between these divine encounters because they offer unique insights into the nature of God's revelation. Angel appearances convey God's messages and interventions through His messengers. Christophanies reveal the pre-incarnate presence of Jesus, bridging the Old and New Testaments. Theophanies showcase God's direct and overwhelming presence, emphasising His holiness and transcendence.

Understanding these distinctions enriches our comprehension of the biblical narrative's multifaceted ways God interacts with humanity. Whether through angels, Christophanies, or Theophanies, each encounter conveys a profound aspect of God's character and His desire to communicate with His creation.

## Understanding the Orders of Angels and Demons in Scripture

ANGELS AND DEMONS, beings of the spiritual realm, play significant roles in the biblical narrative. Both angelic and demonic entities are organised into various orders or hierarchies, each with distinct functions and purposes. This chapter explores the different orders of angels and demons in Scripture, shedding light on their roles, appearances, and interactions with the human realm.

### Orders of Angels

**Seraphim:** The Seraphim are celestial beings mentioned in Isaiah's vision of God's throne (Isaiah 6:1-3). They are described as having six wings and are fervently devoted to worship, continuously singing, "Holy, holy, holy is the Lord of hosts." Their primary function is to praise and glorify God, reflecting His holiness and majesty.

**Cherubim:** Cherubim are often associated with guarding sacred spaces and objects. Their most well-known role is guarding the entrance to the Garden of Eden after Adam and Eve's expulsion

(Genesis 3:24). In the design of the Ark of the Covenant, two cherubim with outstretched wings adorned the mercy seat (Exodus 25:18-22). Cherubim symbolise God's presence and guardianship.

**Thrones, Dominions, and Powers:** These orders of angels are mentioned in Colossians 1:16 and Ephesians 1:21 as part of the angelic hierarchy. Their specific roles are less explicitly defined in Scripture. Still, they are often associated with the governance and administration of the cosmos.

**Principalities and Archangels:** Principalities and Archangels are high-ranking angels. As mentioned in Romans 8:38, principals appear to have authority over regions or nations. Archangels, such as Michael (Jude 1:9), are known for their roles in significant events, including spiritual warfare and the resurrection of the dead.

**Angels and Ministering Spirits:** Angels, or "messengers," are the Bible's most common order of angels. They serve as intermediaries between God and humanity, delivering messages, providing guidance, and offering protection. Hebrews 1:14 describes them as "ministering spirits sent forth to serve for the sake of those who are to inherit salvation."

### 2. Orders of Demons

**Unclean Spirits:** Unclean spirits are frequently mentioned in the New Testament. They are often associated with illness, possession, and impurity. In Mark 5:1-20, Jesus encounters a man possessed by a legion of unclean spirits, highlighting their destructive and tormenting nature.

**Evil Spirits and Demons:** The New Testament refers to various evil spirits and demons responsible for afflictions and possession. In Luke 7:21, Jesus cured many plagued by unclean spirits, showing their malevolent influence. In the demoniac encounter in Matthew 8:28-34, Jesus cast demons out of two men and into a herd of pigs.

**Rulers, Authorities, Powers of This Dark World:** Ephesians 6:12 speaks of spiritual forces of evil in the heavenly realms, often understood as fallen angels or demonic entities. These "rulers," "authorities," and "powers" are part of Satan's rebellion against God and are engaged in spiritual warfare against believers.

**Legion and the Prince of Demons:** The Gospels describe a specific demoniac identified as "Legion," indicating the presence of many demons in one person (Mark 5:1-20). In Matthew 12:24, the Pharisees accused Jesus of casting out demons by the power of "Beelzebul," often interpreted as a reference to the "Prince of Demons."

**Satanic Hierarchy:** Though not explicitly delineated in Scripture, some Christian traditions have suggested a hierarchy of demons, with Satan as their leader. This hierarchy includes fallen angels who followed Satan in his rebellion against God.

### 3. The Angelic-Demonic Interaction

Throughout Scripture, interactions between angels and demons occur, often within spiritual warfare. The story of the Archangel Michael contending with the Devil over the body of Moses (Jude 1:9) highlights this celestial conflict. In Daniel 10:13, an angelic messenger sent to Daniel is delayed for 21 days by "the prince of the kingdom of Persia," likely a reference to a demonic entity opposing God's plan.

### 4. Theological Considerations

Understanding the orders of angels and demons is a matter of theological curiosity. It carries profound implications for the Christian worldview. It highlights the reality of a spiritual realm that influences human existence. This understanding can deepen one's appreciation of the cosmic battle between good and evil, the significance of spiritual warfare and the protection offered by God's angels.

### 5. The Role of Angels in Redemption

Angels play pivotal roles in the narrative of salvation. They announce the birth of Jesus to the shepherds (Luke 2:8-14), minister to Him in the wilderness (Matthew 4:11), and proclaim His resurrection (Matthew 28:2-7). Angels are witnesses to the unfolding of God's redemptive plan.

### 6. The Consequences of Demonic Influence

Conversely, the influence of demons is evident in the brokenness of the world. They lead people into temptation, possess individuals, and spread spiritual darkness. The New Testament portrays Jesus as the ultimate authority over demonic forces, delivering individuals from their grip.

• • • •

THE ORDERS OF ANGELS and demons provide a deeper understanding of the intricate spiritual realm that operates alongside our physical world. They reveal these celestial beings' multifaceted roles and responsibilities, whether in worship, protection, guidance, or spiritual conflict. Recognising the angelic hierarchy and the presence of demonic forces in Scripture enriches our comprehension of the profound spiritual realities in the biblical narrative and the broader Christian faith.

# Chapter 1: Understanding Angels and Demons

Angels, as portrayed in the Christian Bible, are celestial beings with a divine origin, created by God to serve various roles in the spiritual and physical realms. These messengers of God have fascinated believers and non-believers alike, and their nature, characteristics, and roles are richly detailed throughout the Scriptures.

## Created Beings

ANGELS ARE CREATED beings, brought into existence by God Himself. The Bible does not provide a specific account of the moment of their creation. Still, it does affirm their status as divine entities. The book of Psalms declares, "Praise him, all his angels; praise him, all his heavenly hosts" (Psalm 148:2). This verse acknowledges their celestial existence as part of God's heavenly assembly.

Unlike humans, angels are not born or procreated. They are described as heavenly hosts, implying many angelic beings. In the book of Revelation, John's vision reveals the heavenly scene with myriads of angels surrounding the throne of God, singing His praises (Revelation 5:11-12). This multitude highlights the innumerable nature of these celestial creatures.

## Divine Messengers and Servants

THE PRIMARY ROLE OF angels in the Bible is to act as divine messengers and servants of God. The term "angel" itself is derived from the Greek word "angelos," which means "messenger." This designation reflects their core function of delivering God's messages and carrying out His will.

Angels appear as messengers throughout the Old and New Testaments to deliver important announcements and revelations. In the Old Testament, the angel Gabriel delivers messages to the prophet

Daniel (Daniel 9:21-22) and Mary, foretelling the birth of Jesus (Luke 1:26-38). Angels also played a pivotal role in announcing the birth of Jesus to the shepherds, proclaiming, "I bring you good news that will cause great joy for all the people" (Luke 2:10).

In addition to their role as messengers, angels are portrayed as servants who carry out God's divine will. For example, angels served as agents of God's judgment in destroying Sodom and Gomorrah (Genesis 19:1-26). In the book of Acts, an angel freed the apostles from prison, illustrating their role in delivering believers from danger (Acts 5:19-20).

## Agents of Protection

ANGELS ALSO SERVE AS agents of protection for individuals and nations. The Bible frequently presents instances where angels shield and safeguard God's people. One of the most well-known references to angelic protection is in the book of Psalms, which writes, "For he will command his angels concerning you to guard you in all your ways" (Psalm 91:11).

In the Old Testament, we see the story of Daniel in the lions' den, where God sent an angel to protect him from harm (Daniel 6:22). The angel's intervention preserved Daniel's life, demonstrating the protective nature of these celestial beings. Similarly, when the prophet Elisha and his servant were surrounded by an enemy army, the servant saw the mountains filled with horses and chariots of fire, signifying the presence of angelic protection (2 Kings 6:15-17).

## Instruments of Worship

ANGELS PLAY A SIGNIFICANT role in heavenly worship, as they are often depicted as participating in adoration and praise of God. The book of Revelation provides a glimpse into the heavenly scene, where myriads of angels, along with the living creatures and elders, worship the Lamb of God:

"And I heard every creature in heaven and on earth and under the earth and in the sea, and all that is in them, saying, 'To him who sits on the throne and to the Lamb be blessing and honour and glory and might forever and ever!'" (Revelation 5:13)

This portrayal emphasises the angelic role as worshipers of the Almighty, perpetually praising Him in the celestial realms.

## Divine Warriors

IN CERTAIN BIBLICAL narratives, angels are depicted as divine warriors who engage in spiritual battles. The book of Daniel provides an example of this role, where the angelic being who visited Daniel faced opposition from a demonic force, described as the "prince of the kingdom of Persia" (Daniel 10:13). This narrative hints at the unseen cosmic battles that take place in the heavenly realms.

In the New Testament, angels are seen as part of the celestial army of God. In the book of Revelation, Michael and his angels wage war against the dragon and his angels (Revelation 12:7). This imagery emphasises the concept of angelic warriors defending the divine order against the forces of darkness.

## Incorporeal and Glorious Beings

ANGELS ARE OFTEN DESCRIBED as incorporeal or spiritual beings. Unlike humans, they do not possess physical bodies yet can take on temporary corporeal forms when interacting with humans. In the Bible, they are frequently described as beings of light and glory.

The appearance of angels is awe-inspiring and radiant, causing fear and amazement in those who encounter them. When the angel appeared to the shepherds to announce the birth of Jesus, the glory of the Lord shone around them. They were filled with fear (Luke 2:9). The appearance of angels often serves as a reminder of their mission's divine and holy nature.

## Genderless Beings

IN THE BIBLE, ANGELS are not ascribed a specific gender. They are often referred to using masculine pronouns in English translations, but this is primarily for linguistic convenience. The Bible does not provide explicit information regarding the gender of angels.

Angels are frequently described using the term "sons of God" (Job 1:6, Job 2:1) or simply as "angels." This gender-neutral terminology indicates that their nature transcends human concepts of gender.

## Approachable Yet Powerful

WHILE ANGELS ARE GLORIOUS and powerful beings, the Bible portrays them as approachable. They interact with humans in a manner that conveys both power and comfort. When the angel appeared to Mary, he greeted her with the words, "Do not be afraid" (Luke 1:30), offering reassurance even in the face of their celestial presence.

The dual nature of angels as both powerful and approachable emphasises their role as intermediaries between the divine and human realms. They serve as messengers, protectors, and guides, bridging the gap between the transcendent God and His creation.

• • • •

AS DEPICTED IN THE Christian Bible, the nature of angels is one of divine, created, and incorporeal beings who serve as messengers, protectors, worshipers, and divine warriors. Their roles encompass various functions, reflecting their position as part of God's heavenly hosts. Understanding their nature is essential to appreciate their significance in the biblical narrative and their impact on the lives of believers. The following sections will explore the various aspects of angels' roles, including their appearances in the Old and New Testaments and their relevance for contemporary believers.

# The Nature of Demons

As we explore the realm of angels and demons from a Christian Bible perspective, it is crucial to explore the nature and characteristics of demons. The Bible provides glimpses into these malevolent spiritual entities, shedding light on their origins, activities, and impact on the lives of believers.

## Fallen Angels

THE NATURE OF DEMONS is intricately tied to their origin, as they were not created as demonic beings but were initially angels who rebelled against God. The most prominent figure among these fallen angels is Lucifer, who became Satan, the adversary of God and humanity.

The book of Isaiah provides a glimpse into Lucifer's rebellion and fall:

"How you are fallen from heaven, O Day Star, son of Dawn! How you are cut down to the ground, you who laid the nations low! You said in your heart, 'I will ascend to heaven; above the stars of God, I will set my throne on high; I will sit on the mount of assembly in the far reaches of the north; I will ascend above the heights of the clouds; I will make myself like the Most High.' But you are brought down to Sheol, to the far reaches of the pit." (Isaiah 14:12-15)

This passage highlights the pride and rebellion that led to Lucifer's fall and transformation into Satan. Lucifer was originally a beautiful and powerful angel. Still, his rebellion against God led to his expulsion from the heavenly realm.

## Malevolent Spirits

DEMONS, AS THE FALLEN angels who follow Satan, are malevolent and maleficent in nature. Their activities are characterised by deception, oppression, and harm. The New Testament contains numerous accounts of demonic possession, where individuals are tormented by these malevolent spirits.

One such account is found in Mark 5:1-20, where a man possessed by a legion of demons lived among the tombs, crying out and inflicting harm upon himself. The presence of demons within him led to severe suffering and isolation. This narrative illustrates the destructive influence of demons on human lives.

## Agents of Deception

DEMONS ARE PORTRAYED in the Bible as agents of deception and falsehood. The apostle Paul warns of "seducing spirits" and "doctrines of devils" in his first letter to Timothy (1 Timothy 4:1). These malevolent spirits seek to lead people away from the truth and into error.

In the book of 2 Corinthians, Paul acknowledges the danger of deception posed by Satan and his minions:

"And no wonder, for even Satan disguises himself as an angel of light. So, it is no surprise that his servants also disguise themselves as servants of righteousness. Their end will correspond to their deeds." (2 Corinthians 11:14-15)

This passage emphasises the subtlety of demonic deception, as they can masquerade as beings of light while spreading falsehood and confusion.

## Unclean Spirits

DEMONS ARE OFTEN REFERRED to in the Bible as "unclean spirits." This designation points to their impurity and moral corruption. In the New Testament, Jesus encounters numerous individuals possessed by unclean spirits. These spirits caused physical, emotional, and spiritual distress, rendering individuals unclean and separated from society.

In Luke 4:33-36, Jesus casts out an unclean spirit from a man, demonstrating His authority over these malevolent entities. The passage highlights the defiling nature of unclean spirits and the need for deliverance from their influence.

## Afflictors of the Body and Mind

DEMONS ARE FREQUENTLY associated with the affliction of the human body and mind. In the New Testament, we encounter individuals who are not only possessed by demons but also suffer from various physical and psychological ailments as a result. This dual affliction emphasises the oppressive and tormenting nature of demonic possession.

For example, in Matthew 17:14-18, a man brings his demon-possessed son to Jesus, explaining that the demon not only seizes the boy but also throws him into fire and water. The possession results in physical harm and suffering, demonstrating the harmful impact of demons on the human condition.

Similarly, in the book of Mark, a man possessed by an unclean spirit in a synagogue cried out, causing both physical and emotional distress (Mark 1:23-26). These accounts reveal the multifaceted nature of demonic influence on human lives.

## Association with Pagan Practices

DEMONS ARE ALSO ASSOCIATED with pagan practices and idolatry in the Bible. The Old Testament frequently warns against engaging in practices that involve worshipping false gods and idols, which can lead to contact with malevolent spiritual forces.

In Deuteronomy 32:16-17, the Israelites are cautioned about turning to foreign gods:

"They stirred him to jealousy with strange gods; with abominations, they provoked him to anger. They sacrificed to demons that were no gods, to gods they had never known, to new gods that had come recently, whom your fathers had never dreaded."

This passage emphasises the danger of idolatry and its association with demons. It serves as a reminder of the need for monotheistic worship and devotion to the one true God.

## Prowlers and Seekers

THE BIBLE ALSO PORTRAYS demons as prowlers and seekers. In the New Testament, Jesus shares a parable about an unclean spirit that leaves a person but returns to find the person's "house" (the individual) unoccupied, then brings along seven other spirits more wicked than itself (Matthew 12:43-45). This parable illustrates the persistent and seeking nature of demons.

Demons are not content with remaining idle but actively seeking opportunities to afflict and influence human lives. Their restlessness and malevolence are demonstrated in their actions and their relentless pursuit of harming individuals.

## Powers and Principalities

IN ADDITION TO INDIVIDUAL demons, the New Testament mentions powers and principalities in the spiritual realm. These terms refer to high-ranking demonic entities that influence regions and nations. The apostle Paul addresses this concept in his letter to the Ephesians:

"For we do not wrestle against flesh and blood, but against the rulers, against the authorities, against the cosmic powers over this present darkness, against the spiritual forces of evil in the heavenly places." (Ephesians 6:12)

This passage highlights the hierarchical and influential nature of demonic powers and principalities in the spiritual realm. Believers are engaged in a spiritual battle against these malevolent entities.

## Seeking to Devour and Destroy

THE BIBLE WARNS THAT demons, under the leadership of Satan, seek to devour and destroy. In 1 Peter 5:8, believers are cautioned to be vigilant:

"Be sober-minded; be watchful. Your adversary, the devil, prowls around like a roaring lion, seeking someone to devour."

This imagery emphasises the predatory and destructive nature of demons and Satan. Their ultimate goal is to lead people away from God, spread deception, and cause harm and destruction.

• • • •

THE NATURE OF DEMONS, as depicted in the Christian Bible, is one of fallen angels who have rebelled against God and become malevolent spirits. They are agents of deception, unclean and defiling spirits, prowlers, and seekers of rest, and they seek to afflict and torment humanity. The Bible portrays demons as powerful, destructive entities under the leadership of Satan, with the ability to influence and oppress both individuals and regions.

Understanding the nature of demons is essential for believers as it provides insights into their spiritual battles and challenges. Demonic influence and deception can lead individuals away from the truth and into spiritual bondage. Recognising the malevolent nature of these entities is the first step in guarding against their influence.

As we continue our exploration in the following chapters, we will explore the biblical narratives that illustrate encounters with demons and the consequences of their influence on human lives. We will also discuss the believer's role in resisting and overcoming the forces of darkness, emphasising the importance of spiritual discernment, prayer, and the "Armor of God" as tools for protection and deliverance in the unseen struggle against these malevolent entities.

Establishing a firm biblical foundation is essential to comprehend the intricate world of angels and demons from a Christian Bible perspective. The Scriptures provide the primary source of knowledge about these spiritual entities, offering insights into their roles, interactions with humanity, and the broader cosmic context in which they operate.

## Angels in the Bible

ANGELS ARE PROMINENT figures throughout the Old and New Testaments of the Bible. Their appearances are woven into the narrative, serving as messengers, protectors, worshipers, and instruments of divine will. Let's explore some key biblical references that underpin our understanding of angels:

- **Angel Appearing to Hagar (Genesis 16:7-14):** In this early account, an angel encounters Hagar, fleeing from her mistress, Sarai. The angel delivers a message from God and provides assurance and guidance to Hagar. This incident illustrates the role of angels as divine messengers.
- **The Angels Visiting Abraham (Genesis 18:1-15):** Angels visit Abraham to deliver the news of the birth of Isaac, Sarah's laughter, and the impending judgment on Sodom and Gomorrah. This narrative emphasises the significance of angels in conveying important messages, foretelling future events, and executing divine judgment.
- **Angels at the Birth of Jesus (Luke 2:8-15):** Perhaps one of the most well-known angelic appearances, this passage recounts the angel's announcement of the birth of Jesus to the shepherds. The glory of the Lord shines around them, and

many angels join in praise. This event highlights the role of angels in heralding significant moments in God's redemptive plan.

- **Angels at the Empty Tomb (Matthew 28:1-10):** Following Jesus' resurrection, angels appear at the empty tomb, delivering the news of His resurrection to the women who had come to anoint His body. This demonstrates the angelic role in witnessing the pivotal event of Christ's victory over death.

- **Angels Ministering to Jesus (Matthew 4:11):** After His temptation in the wilderness, angels minister to Jesus. This incident showcases the support and care angels provide even to the Son of God during His earthly ministry.

These references provide a solid biblical foundation for the roles and functions of angels. They serve as divine messengers, guardians, and worshipers who participate in significant events within the biblical narrative.

## Demons in the Bible

AS MALEVOLENT SPIRITUAL entities, demons are also encountered in various biblical passages. Their activities involve deception, affliction, and spiritual oppression. Here are some key biblical references that contribute to our understanding of demons:

- **Demon-Possessed Man (Mark 5:1-20):** This narrative tells the story of a man possessed by a legion of demons who lived among the tombs and tormented himself. Jesus casts out the demons, demonstrating His authority over them. This account illustrates the destructive power of demons and the freedom that Jesus offers from their oppression.

- **Demons Recognising Jesus (Mark 1:21-28):** In this passage, a man with an unclean spirit recognises Jesus as the "Holy One of God." Jesus rebukes the demon, and it leaves the man. This demonstrates that even demons acknowledge the authority and holiness of Jesus.

- **Paul's Encounter with a Fortune-Telling Spirit (Acts 16:16-18):** While in Philippi, Paul and Silas encounter a slave girl possessed by a spirit of divination. Paul commands the spirit to come out of her, freeing her from its influence. This incident shows how demons can empower individuals to engage in practices that oppose the gospel's message.

- **Paul's Thorn in the Flesh (2 Corinthians 12:7):** Paul mentions a "thorn in the flesh" that tormented him, sent by a "messenger of Satan." While the nature of this thorn is not explicitly identified, it highlights the idea that demonic affliction or opposition can impact even faithful believers.

- **Demonic Powers and Principalities (Ephesians 6:12):** In his letter to the Ephesians, Paul speaks of the believer's struggle, not against flesh and blood but against "the rulers, against the authorities, against the cosmic powers over this present darkness, against the spiritual forces of evil in the heavenly places." This passage emphasises the hierarchical nature of demonic powers in the spiritual realm.

These references offer a foundational understanding of the malevolent nature and activities of demons in the biblical narrative. They are portrayed as agents of deception, torment, and opposition to God's purposes.

## The Unseen Cosmic Battle

THE UNSEEN COSMIC BATTLE in the heavenly realms is central to our understanding of angels and demons. This battle is alluded to in various biblical passages and is a crucial component of the broader spiritual context.

The apostle Paul, in his letter to the Ephesians, vividly describes this cosmic struggle:

"For we do not wrestle against flesh and blood, but against the rulers, against the authorities, against the cosmic powers over this present darkness, against the spiritual forces of evil in the heavenly places." (Ephesians 6:12)

This verse emphasises the existence of powerful spiritual entities engaged in a cosmic battle between good and evil. The believer's spiritual warfare is not a metaphorical or symbolic concept but a real and ongoing conflict.

The book of Revelation also provides glimpses into this cosmic battle. In Revelation 12, John's vision includes a war in heaven, where Michael and his angels fight against the dragon (Satan) and his angels. This celestial conflict has profound implications for the earthly realm and the lives of believers.

Understanding the cosmic battle is essential for grasping the broader context in which angels and demons operate. It emphasises the spiritual warfare believers are part of and the need for spiritual discernment, protection, and reliance on God's power in the face of this unseen struggle.

## The Consequences for Believers

THE BIBLICAL NARRATIVE'S presence of angels and demons carries significant consequences for believers. These consequences encompass spiritual warfare, the need for discernment, and the reliance on the "Armor of God" for protection.

As mentioned in Ephesians 6:12, believers are engaged in spiritual warfare against the forces of evil in the heavenly realms. This warfare is not a passive experience but an active and ongoing battle. It requires vigilance, prayer, and the utilisation of spiritual resources to stand firm in faith.

The presence of demonic forces also highlights the importance of spiritual discernment. Believers must be able to recognise the influence of demons and guard against deception. The apostle John cautions against believing every spirit, instructing believers to "test the spirits to see whether they are from God, for many false prophets have gone out into the world" (1 John 4:1). This discernment is crucial to avoid falling into deception and false teachings.

The biblical foundation we have established emphasises the vital role of the "Armor of God" in defending against the schemes of the devil and his demonic forces. The apostle Paul, in Ephesians 6:10-18, provides a detailed description of this spiritual armour, including the belt of truth, the breastplate of righteousness, shoes of the gospel of peace, the shield of faith, the helmet of salvation, and the sword of the Spirit (the Word of God). Each component is a defensive or offensive tool in the believer's battle against spiritual adversaries.

Incorporating this spiritual armour into one's daily life is essential for withstanding the attacks and temptations of the enemy. It is a protective shield and a powerful weapon in the ongoing spiritual struggle.

## The Relevance for Believers Today

THE BIBLICAL FOUNDATIONS regarding angels and demons are not confined to ancient texts but continue to hold profound relevance for believers today. Understanding the nature and roles of these spiritual entities and the cosmic battle in which they are engaged provides a framework for comprehending the spiritual challenges and victories that contemporary Christians may encounter.

The presence of angels as messengers, protectors, and worshipers is a source of comfort and assurance for believers. Though not explicitly detailed in the Bible, the belief in guardian angels has brought solace to many who see these celestial beings as instruments of divine protection and guidance.

Conversely, the recognition of demonic forces emphasises the reality of spiritual warfare in the lives of believers. The accounts of demon possession, oppression, and deception in the New Testament serve as cautionary tales, highlighting the need for discernment, prayer, and the utilisation of the "Armor of God" to withstand the schemes of the enemy.

The biblical foundation also reminds believers of the unseen cosmic battle in the heavenly realms. This battle is not distant but directly impacts the lives of individuals and nations. Awareness of this ongoing struggle is crucial for equipping believers to stand firm and confidently engage in spiritual warfare.

In conclusion, the biblical foundations regarding angels and demons provide a solid framework for understanding these spiritual entities and their impact on the lives of believers. The Scriptures offer rich insights into their nature, roles, and the cosmic context in which they operate. This understanding is not relegated to the past. Still, it remains profoundly relevant for contemporary Christians, equipping them to navigate the unseen struggle and remain steadfast in their faith. As we explore the world of angels and demons in subsequent chapters, we will explore specific narratives and practical applications of these foundational truths.

36

# Angelic Appearances in the Old Testament

The Old Testament is replete with accounts of angelic appearances, where these celestial messengers play significant roles in God's interactions with humanity. These encounters provide valuable insights into the nature and functions of angels, offering a rich tapestry of divine messages, guidance, and protection. Let us explore some of these remarkable Old Testament instances.

## The Angelic Encounter of Hagar (Genesis 16:7-14)

THE STORY OF HAGAR, Sarah's Egyptian maidservant, is one of the earliest recorded encounters with an angel in the Old Testament. Hagar found herself in a distressing situation, having fled from her mistress due to mistreatment. In the wilderness, an angel of the Lord appeared to her.

The angel addressed Hagar by name and inquired about her situation. He then delivered a divine message, promising her descendants too numerous to count. This angelic encounter provided comfort and direction to Hagar, who responded with reverence, calling the name of the Lord who spoke to her "El-Roi," meaning "the God who sees."

This account demonstrates the role of angels as messengers and comforters, intervening in the lives of individuals in times of distress.

## Abraham's Visitors (Genesis 18:1-15)

ABRAHAM'S ENCOUNTER with three visitors near the oaks of Mamre is a well-known and pivotal narrative in the Old Testament. While the text initially refers to them as "men," it becomes evident that these visitors are angels, and one of them is likely the Lord Himself.

The angels bring a message of promise to Abraham and Sarah, foretelling the birth of Isaac. This visitation also serves as a prelude to the announcement of divine judgment on Sodom and Gomorrah, revealing the angels' role in conveying blessings and warnings.

Abraham's hospitality towards these celestial beings highlights their ability to take on human form and interact with humanity. This encounter emphasises the dual function of angels as messengers of blessings and agents of divine judgment.

## Jacob's Wrestling with the Angel (Genesis 32:22-32)

JACOB'S ENCOUNTER WITH an angel is a unique and enigmatic passage in the Old Testament. As Jacob wrestles with an unidentified man by the Jabbok River, it becomes apparent that this "man" is a divine being, often interpreted as an angel.

The wrestling match symbolises Jacob's struggle, both with the angel and with his own past. As the night progresses, Jacob refuses to release the angel until he receives a blessing. In response, the angel touches Jacob's hip, resulting in a lifelong limp. He blesses him by changing his name to Israel, signifying his transformation from "deceiver" to "he who struggles with God."

This encounter showcases the symbolic and transformative nature of angelic interactions. It signifies not only the physical but also the spiritual impact of such encounters on individuals.

## The Angelic Appearance to Joshua (Joshua 5:13-15)

AS THE ISRAELITES PREPARED to conquer Jericho, Joshua had a remarkable encounter with a "commander of the army of the Lord." This divine figure, often called an angel, appeared to Joshua near Jericho.

Upon seeing the angel, Joshua fell facedown in reverence and inquired if he was for Israel or for their adversaries. The angel identified Himself as the commander of the Lord's army and instructed Joshua to remove his sandals, as the ground he stood on was holy.

This encounter reassured Joshua and prepared him for the conquest of Jericho. It emphasises the role of angels as divine guides and protectors in times of conflict and warfare.

## The Angelic Message to Gideon (Judges 6:11-24)

GIDEON'S ENCOUNTER with an angelic messenger is a testament to God's call upon unlikely individuals. Gideon was threshing wheat in a winepress, attempting to hide from the Midianites when the angel of the Lord appeared to him.

The angel addressed Gideon as a "mighty man of valour" and delivered a message of divine commission, instructing him to lead Israel in defeating the Midianites. Gideon initially questioned the angel's message and sought a sign granted through a miraculous offering.

This encounter illustrates the angel's role in delivering divine assignments and encouraging individuals to fulfil their God-given destinies. It emphasises the transformative power of angelic encounters in the lives of ordinary people.

## The Angelic Announcement to Manoah and His Wife (Judges 13:2-23)

THE BIRTH OF SAMSON, one of the judges of Israel, was foretold through an angelic visitation to Manoah and his wife, who were barren. In this Old Testament account, an angel appeared to Manoah's wife and later to Him.

The angel delivered the message of Samson's birth and his future consecration as a Nazirite. In response to Manoah's request, the angel reiterated the instructions and revealed His name as "Wonderful." The angel's ascension in the altar's flame was a sign to Manoah and his wife.

This angelic announcement highlights the role of angels in foretelling significant events and guiding individuals in fulfilling divine purposes. This angelic message resulted from Samson's life, which was marked by divine strength.

## Daniel's Encounters with Angelic Beings (Daniel 9:20-27, Daniel 10:1-21)

THE BOOK OF DANIEL contains several encounters with angelic beings. In Daniel 9, the prophet prays fervently for the restoration of Jerusalem and the forgiveness of Israel's sins. In response, the angel Gabriel appears to Daniel and provides insights into the future, including the prophecy of the seventy weeks.

In Daniel 10, Daniel has a profound encounter with a glorious angelic being. This encounter leaves Daniel weakened and in awe. The angel reveals that he had been delayed by a spiritual battle with the "prince of the kingdom of Persia" and the future involvement of the "prince of Greece."

These encounters with angelic beings in the Book of Daniel showcase the angels' role in delivering prophetic messages and engaging in cosmic battles in the heavenly realms.

## The Angelic Deliverance of Peter (Acts 12:6-11)

IN THE NEW TESTAMENT, the apostle Peter's miraculous escape from prison with the help of an angel is a remarkable example of divine intervention. While Peter was imprisoned by King Herod, an angel of the Lord appeared, causing Peter's chains to fall off and leading him to freedom.

Peter initially thought he was experiencing a vision, but the angel's intervention was real. This incident demonstrates the angel's role as a deliverer, rescuing believers from dire situations.

These Old Testament angelic encounters illustrate the multifaceted nature of angels as divine messengers, comforters, guides, and protectors. They highlight the importance of faith, obedience, and receptivity to divine messages in human interactions with celestial beings. These accounts are not merely historical narratives but offer timeless lessons about the roles of angels in the lives of believers, emphasising their significance in both ancient times and the contemporary faith of Christians.

## Key Takeaways from Old Testament Angelic Appearances

AS WE REFLECT ON THESE angelic appearances in the Old Testament, several key takeaways emerge:

1. **Messengers of God:** Angels consistently serve as messengers of God, delivering divine revelations, promises, and instructions to individuals. These encounters highlight their role in conveying God's will to humanity.
2. **Comforters in Distress:** Angelic appearances often occur in distress, offering comfort, assurance, and guidance. Hagar, Abraham, and Manoah's wife found solace and direction in their encounters with angels during challenging circumstances.
3. **Guides and Protectors:** Angels are divine guides and protectors, as seen in Joshua's encounter with the commander of the Lord's army. They provide guidance and assistance, especially in moments of conflict or decision-making.
4. **Transformative Encounters:** Angelic interactions have the power to transform individuals. Jacob's wrestling with the angel resulted in a name and identity change, symbolising spiritual transformation. Gideon's encounter transformed him from a timid individual into a mighty leader.
5. **Prophetic Revelations:** Angels frequently deliver prophetic messages, foretelling future events and God's plans. Daniel's encounters with angelic beings offer profound insights into the unfolding of history and the spiritual battles in the heavenly realms.
6. **Deliverers from Bondage:** The story of Peter's miraculous

escape from prison showcases angels as deliverers who intervene to rescue believers from seemingly insurmountable situations.

These Old Testament angelic appearances lay the foundation for understanding the roles and functions of angels in the broader biblical narrative. They highlight the diverse ways angels interact with humanity, offering divine guidance, protection, and messages that transcend the boundaries of time and culture.

As we journey through the subsequent chapters of this exploration, we will continue to uncover the significance of angelic encounters in the Old and New Testaments, providing a comprehensive understanding of the celestial messengers and their relevance to believers today.

# Angelic Appearances in the New Testament

The New Testament continues the rich tradition of angelic encounters found in the Old Testament. In this era, angels played a pivotal role in announcing the birth of Jesus, providing guidance and protection, and delivering messages that shaped the early Christian community. Let us explore some of the most significant angelic appearances in the New Testament, which contribute to a deeper understanding of the roles and functions of these celestial beings.

## The Angelic Announcements of Jesus' Birth

THE NEW TESTAMENT OPENS with the miraculous announcements of the births of John the Baptist and Jesus, both of which involve angelic appearances.

- **The Announcement to Zechariah (Luke 1:5-25):** The angel Gabriel appears to Zechariah, a priest, while he is in the temple performing his priestly duties. Gabriel delivers the news of the upcoming birth of John the Baptist despite Zechariah and his wife Elizabeth's elderly age. The angelic message serves as a prelude to the birth of the forerunner of Jesus and emphasises God's divine plan.
- **The Announcement to Mary (Luke 1:26-38):** Gabriel appears to Mary, a virgin from Nazareth, after encountering Zechariah. The angel announces that she will conceive and give birth to the Messiah, Jesus. Mary's humility and submission to God's plan are evident in her response, "I am the Lord's servant; may your word to me be fulfilled." This angelic visitation marks the beginning of Jesus' earthly ministry.

# The Angelic Guidance and Protection of the Holy Family

THE HOLY FAMILY, CONSISTING of Joseph, Mary, and the infant Jesus, received divine guidance and protection through angelic appearances.

- **The Angelic Dream to Joseph (Matthew 1:18-25):** In a dream, an angel of the Lord appears to Joseph, revealing Mary's miraculous pregnancy and assuring him of God's divine plan. The angel instructs Joseph to take Mary as his wife and names the child Jesus, signifying His role as the Savior of humanity. This angelic visitation affirms Joseph's role in protecting and raising Jesus.

- **The Angelic Warning and Flight to Egypt (Matthew 2:13-15):** After the visit of the Magi and the revelation of Herod's sinister intentions, an angel appears to Joseph in another dream, instructing him to take the child Jesus and Mary and flee to Egypt. The angel's message serves as a critical warning and protection, preserving the life of the young Messiah.

- **The Angelic Return to Nazareth (Matthew 2:19-23):** Following Herod's death, an angel directs Joseph to return to the land of Israel with Jesus and Mary. This angelic guidance ensures that the Holy Family safely returns to their homeland, fulfilling the prophecies about Jesus being called a Nazarene.

These angelic encounters in the early life of Jesus highlight the guidance, protection, and divine direction provided by celestial messengers. They emphasise the importance of obedient responses to angelic messages in fulfilling God's purposes.

## The Angels' Proclamation to the Shepherds (Luke 2:8-20)

ONE OF THE MOST CELEBRATED angelic appearances in the New Testament is the proclamation to the shepherds on the night of Jesus' birth. Many heavenly hosts appear to a group of shepherds in the fields, announcing the birth of the Savior in Bethlehem.

The angelic message is filled with joy and celebration, declaring, "Glory to God in the highest, and on earth peace to men on whom his favour rests." The shepherds respond by visiting the newborn Jesus and spreading the news of the angelic proclamation throughout the region.

This angelic appearance signifies the pivotal moment of Jesus' birth, bringing tidings of great joy to humanity. It also emphasises the role of angels as heralds of significant events in God's redemptive plan.

## The Angelic Ministry to Jesus in the Wilderness (Matthew 4:11)

FOLLOWING HIS BAPTISM, Jesus spent 40 days and nights in the wilderness, fasting and being tempted by the devil. After this period, angels come to minister to Him. Although the specific details of this ministry are not provided, the presence of angels signifies their role in providing comfort and sustenance to Jesus during a challenging time.

This brief reference emphasises the compassionate and supportive nature of angels, even in the life of the Son of God. It reminds us of their presence during our own times of testing and difficulty.

## The Angelic Appearance to Zechariah (Luke 1:8-20)

THE NEW TESTAMENT ALSO records an angelic appearance to Zechariah, the father of John the Baptist, who served as a priest in the temple. While Zechariah offered incense, the angel Gabriel appeared to him, delivering a message that his wife Elizabeth would bear a son in their old age, and he should name him John.

Zechariah initially responded with disbelief, and as a result, he was struck mute until the prophecy was fulfilled. This angelic visitation heralded the birth of John the Baptist, who would prepare the way for the coming of Jesus.

## The Angelic Messages to Mary and Joseph (Matthew 1:20-21; Luke 1:30-33)

IN ADDITION TO THE initial announcements to Mary and Joseph, both received subsequent angelic messages that provided guidance and clarification regarding the birth and naming of Jesus.

- **The Angel's Message to Joseph (Matthew 1:20-21):** After Joseph discovers Mary's pregnancy, an angel of the Lord appears to him in a dream. The angel reassures Joseph, confirming the divine nature of the child conceived in Mary. The angel instructs Joseph to name the child Jesus, emphasising His role as the Savior who will save people from their sins.
- **The Angel's Message to Mary (Luke 1:30-33):** While the initial announcement of Jesus' birth occurred in Luke 1:26-38, Mary further affirms her child's divine nature through the angelic message. The angel highlights Jesus' future as a king who will reign over the house of Jacob forever, and His kingdom will have no end.

These angelic messages to Mary and Joseph affirm the unique identity and purpose of Jesus as the Savior and eternal King. They provide clarity and divine guidance in fulfilling their roles in God's redemptive plan.

## The Angelic Appearance at the Tomb (Matthew 28:1-10)

FOLLOWING JESUS' CRUCIFIXION and burial, the angelic appearance at the tomb is a central event in the New Testament. As the women come to the tomb early on the first day of the week, they encounter an angel who has rolled away the stone from the tomb's entrance.

The angel delivers the astonishing news that Jesus has risen from the dead, and he instructs the women to go and tell the disciples. This angelic appearance marks the most significant event in Christian history—the resurrection of Jesus Christ.

The angelic message at the tomb is a source of hope, joy, and confirmation of Jesus' victory over death.

This incredible angelic appearance is a pivotal moment that changed the course of human history. It is a testament to the powerful role of angels in bearing witness to the most profound event in the Christian faith—the resurrection of Christ.

## The Angelic Release of Peter from Prison (Acts 12:6-11)

THE NEW TESTAMENT ALSO records an angelic intervention in the life of the apostle Peter. While Herod imprisoned Peter, an angel of the Lord appeared to him in his cell. The angel's visitation included physical acts such as striking Peter on the side, causing his chains to fall off, and leading him out of the prison.

Initially believing he was experiencing a vision, Peter realised that the angel's intervention was real. He followed the angel, and together, they passed the first and second guards and reached the iron gate leading to the city, which opened miraculously. The angel then departed, and Peter found himself free.

This angelic rescue serves as a powerful example of divine deliverance and intervention. It emphasises the role of angels as agents of God's providence and protection, even in the face of severe adversity.

## Key Takeaways from New Testament Angelic Appearances

REFLECTING ON THESE angelic appearances in the New Testament, several key takeaways emerge:

1. **Announcing the Messiah:** Angels play a central role in announcing the birth of Jesus, emphasising His unique identity as the Savior of humanity. Their messages to Zechariah, Mary, and Joseph provide clarity and assurance regarding the divine nature of Christ.

2. **Guiding and Protecting the Holy Family:** Angelic appearances guide and protect the Holy Family, ensuring the safety of Jesus during His infancy. These encounters highlight the role of angels as guardians and protectors of God's divine plan.

3. **Heralding Good News:** The angelic proclamation to the shepherds and the message at the empty tomb emphasise the role of angels as heralds of significant events in the Christian narrative. They bring tidings of great joy and confirmation of the resurrection.

4. **Ministering to Jesus:** Angels minister to Jesus in the wilderness, demonstrating their role as providers of comfort and sustenance. This ministry emphasises the compassion and care of angels.

5. **Guidance and Warning:** Angelic appearances offer guidance and warnings, as seen in the dreams and visions given to Joseph and the direction provided to the shepherds. These encounters highlight the importance of obedience to angelic

messages.

6. **Deliverance and Intervention:** Angels intervene in human affairs to bring about deliverance and protection. The rescue of Peter from prison illustrates their role as agents of divine providence, even in the face of adversity.

These New Testament angelic appearances not only shape the foundational beliefs of Christianity but also provide timeless lessons about the roles and functions of angels in the lives of believers. They emphasise the divine guidance, protection, and comfort provided by celestial messengers and their significance in unfolding God's redemptive plan.

As we journey through the subsequent chapters of this exploration, we will continue to uncover the profound impact of angelic encounters in both the Old and New Testaments, offering a comprehensive understanding of the celestial messengers and their continued relevance to believers today.

# The Role of Angels in Biblical Narratives

In the rich tapestry of the Bible, angels play a multifaceted role that extends beyond delivering messages or making announcements. They are active participants in God's divine plan, serving as instruments of His will, protectors of the faithful, and witnesses to pivotal moments in human history. This chapter explores the diverse roles of angels in biblical narratives, showcasing their significance in the unfolding drama of salvation.

## Messengers of Divine Revelation

ANGELS ARE RENOWNED as messengers of divine revelation, serving as intermediaries between God and humanity. They convey important messages, prophecies, and revelations to individuals, prophets, and entire communities.

- **The Annunciation to Mary (Luke 1:26-38):** In one of the most iconic angelic announcements, Gabriel appears to Mary, announcing the conception and birth of Jesus. This divine message carries profound implications, as Mary is chosen to be the mother of the Messiah. It is through the angel's revelation that God's redemptive plan is set in motion.
- **The Birth of John the Baptist (Luke 1:5-25):** Gabriel's visit to Zechariah is another instance of angelic revelation. Zechariah is informed that he and his elderly wife, Elizabeth, will have a son named John, who will prepare the way for the Lord. This message serves to announce the birth of the forerunner to the Messiah.
- **The Revelation of the Empty Tomb (Matthew 28:1-10):** Angels are central in revealing the resurrection of Jesus. At the empty tomb, they proclaim the good news to the women

who have come to anoint Jesus' body. The message of the resurrection, delivered by angels, is a pivotal moment in Christian history.

These angelic messages convey divine purposes, enact God's will, and guide the faithful towards their roles in God's redemptive plan. They emphasise the importance of angelic mediation in the unfolding drama of salvation.

## Agents of Divine Intervention

ANGELS FREQUENTLY ACT as agents of divine intervention, affecting miraculous changes in human circumstances. They provide guidance, protection, and deliverance to those in need.

- **Protection of the Holy Baby (Matthew 2:13-15):** Following the Magi's visit, an angel appears to Joseph in a dream, instructing him to flee to Egypt with Mary and the infant Jesus to escape Herod's murderous plot. This angelic intervention ensures the safety of Jesus Christ. It fulfils Old Testament prophecies regarding the Messiah's sojourn in Egypt.
- **The Release of Peter from Prison (Acts 12:6-11):** In a moment of crisis, when Peter is imprisoned and guarded by soldiers, an angel of the Lord appears. The angel's intervention includes striking Peter on the side, causing his chains to fall off, and leading him out of the prison. Initially believing it was a vision, Peter realises he has been miraculously freed.
- **Rescue of Lot and His Family (Genesis 19:15-22):** In the narrative of Sodom and Gomorrah, angels intervene to save Lot and his family from the impending destruction. The

angels urge Lot to flee the city before its judgment, illustrating their role in providing protection and guidance in peril.

These instances of angelic intervention demonstrate the supernatural capacity of angels to influence human circumstances. They serve as instruments of God's protection and deliverance, emphasising the divine care and providence at work in the lives of believers.

## Witnesses to Divine Events

ANGELS OFTEN SERVE as witnesses to significant events in the biblical narrative. Their presence emphasises the sacredness and importance of these moments.

- **The Transfiguration (Matthew 17:1-9):** During the transfiguration of Jesus on the mountain, Moses and Elijah appear with Him. Peter, James, and John are witnesses to this extraordinary event. A cloud envelops them, and a voice from the cloud proclaims Jesus as God's beloved Son. The disciples witness this moment, highlighting the divine confirmation of Jesus' identity.
- **The Ascension of Jesus (Acts 1:9-11):** As Jesus ascends to heaven, two men in white robes, understood as angels, appear to the disciples. They assure the disciples that Jesus will return like He ascended. This angelic presence emphasises the event's significance and reassures the disciples.
- **The Resurrection Announcement (Luke 24:1-8):** Angels at the empty tomb are witnesses to the resurrection of Jesus. They announce to the women that Jesus has risen and instruct them to relay the message to the disciples. This

angelic testimony is a crucial element of the resurrection narrative.

The presence of angels as witnesses to these divine events affirms the authenticity and significance of these occurrences. They testify to the divine nature of Jesus and God's redemptive work in human history.

## Comforters in Times of Distress

ANGELS PROVIDE COMFORT and reassurance to individuals in moments of distress and despair. Their presence offers solace and guidance, alleviating fear and anxiety.

- **The Angelic Appearance to Hagar (Genesis 16:7-14):** Hagar, a pregnant maidservant who had fled from her mistress, encounters an angel in the wilderness. The angel provides direction and assures Hagar that God has heard her affliction. This encounter comforts her distressed heart, and she responds by naming the Lord as "the God who sees."

- **The Angelic Ministry to Jesus in the Wilderness (Matthew 4:11):** After His 40-day fast and temptation in the wilderness, angels minister to Jesus. While the specific details of their ministry are not provided, their presence offers comfort and sustenance to Jesus in His moment of physical and spiritual challenge.

- **The Appearance to Elijah (1 Kings 19:1-8):** In a moment of despair, the prophet Elijah flees from the threats of Queen Jezebel. He finds himself in the wilderness, weary and despondent. An angel appears to him, providing food and water, which sustains him for a long journey. This angelic encounter offers comfort and renewal to the discouraged prophet.

These narratives illustrate the role of angels as sources of comfort and support during times of difficulty. They serve as messengers of God's compassion and care, relieving individuals facing physical or emotional challenges.

## Instruments of Divine Judgment

WHILE ANGELS ARE OFTEN associated with delivering messages of grace and hope, they can also serve as instruments of divine judgment.

- **The Destruction of Sodom and Gomorrah (Genesis 19:23-25):** Angels were pivotal in destroying these sinful cities. They visited Lot to warn him of the impending judgment and urged him to flee with his family. When Lot hesitated, the angels seized him and his family, leading them out of the city before it was consumed by fire and brimstone.
- **The Plagues in Egypt (Exodus 12:29-30; Exodus 12:23; Exodus 12:12):** During the Exodus, God used an angel to bring the final plague upon Egypt, leading to the death of the firstborn in households that did not have the blood of the Passover lamb on their doorposts. This event underscored the role of angels in executing God's judgment.

While these instances of divine judgment involve angels, they are carried out under God's righteous purposes. Angels are obedient instruments in executing God's will, whether in judgment or deliverance.

## Protectors of the Faithful

IN VARIOUS BIBLICAL narratives, angels protect the faithful, guarding them from harm and danger.

- **The Commanders of the Lord's Army (Joshua 5:13-15):** When Joshua encounters a commander of the Lord's army near Jericho, it is understood as an angelic presence. This encounter reassures Joshua and the Israelites as they prepare to conquer the Promised Land. The angelic presence emphasises the protection and divine guidance given to the faithful in times of conflict and uncertainty.
- **The Rescue of Daniel from the Lion's Den (Daniel 6:19-23):** In the well-known story of Daniel in the lion's den, an angel is sent to shut the mouths of the hungry lions, sparing Daniel's life. This angelic protection demonstrates God's faithfulness to those who remain steadfast.
- **The Angelic Appearance to the Shepherds (Luke 2:8-20):** At the birth of Jesus, many heavenly hosts appear to shepherds in the fields. Their message is peace and goodwill, serving as a proclamation of the birth of the Savior. The presence of angels at this pivotal moment signifies divine protection and care for the humble and faithful shepherds.

These narratives reveal the protective role of angels in the lives of the faithful. God often dispatched angels to ensure the safety and well-being of those who serve Him faithfully.

## Role in Worship and Praise

ANGELS ARE FREQUENTLY depicted as participants in heavenly worship and praise, underscoring their position as beings created for the adoration and glorification of God.

- **The Heavenly Host at Jesus' Birth (Luke 2:13-14):** At the birth of Jesus, a multitude of heavenly hosts appears, praising God and saying, "Glory to God in the highest, and on earth peace to men on whom his favour rests." These angels engage in adoration and celebration, rejoicing in the incarnation of the Messiah.

- **The Worship of the Seraphim (Isaiah 6:1-3):** Isaiah's vision of the heavenly throne room includes the seraphim, angelic beings who continually cry out, "Holy, holy, holy is the Lord Almighty; the whole earth is full of his glory." These angels are engaged in ceaseless worship and exaltation of God's holiness.

- **The Heavenly Elders and Living Creatures (Revelation 4:8):** In the book of Revelation, we encounter heavenly beings around the throne of God who sing, "Holy, holy, holy is the Lord God Almighty, who was, and is, and is to come." This continuous worship by angelic beings serves as a reminder of God's eternal glory.

The involvement of angels in worship and praise emphasises their eternal reverence for God's majesty and holiness. They set an example of adoration for believers to emulate in their worship.

## Role as Soldiers in Spiritual Warfare

THE BIBLE PORTRAYS angels as participants in spiritual warfare, engaging in battles against demonic forces and cosmic adversaries.

- **The Angelic Struggle in Daniel (Daniel 10:13, 20):** In the book of Daniel, there is a reference to the angel Michael as "one of the chief princes" who comes to assist another angel in a spiritual battle against the "prince of the kingdom of Persia." This narrative provides insight into the cosmic conflict in the heavenly realms, where angels combat spiritual adversaries.

- **The Armour of God (Ephesians 6:10-18):** The apostle Paul instructs believers to put on the "whole armour of God" to withstand the devil's schemes. This spiritual armour includes the belt of truth, breastplate of righteousness, shoes of the gospel of peace, shield of faith, helmet of salvation, and the sword of the Spirit (the Word of God). These components serve as defensive and offensive tools in the believer's battle against spiritual adversaries, emphasising the ongoing spiritual warfare in which angels play a role.

These portrayals of angels in spiritual warfare highlight their active engagement in the cosmic struggle between good and evil. They stand as defenders and allies in the battle against dark forces, working to fulfil God's purposes and protect His people.

## The Silent Observers

IN SOME BIBLICAL NARRATIVES, angels serve as silent observers, witnessing significant events without active participation.

- **The Temptation of Jesus (Matthew 4:1-11):** After Jesus' 40-day fast in the wilderness, Satan tempts Him three times. While angels minister to Jesus after His ordeal, they do not actively intervene during the temptations. Their presence as observers signifies the importance of Jesus' victory over temptation as part of His mission.

- **The Garden of Gethsemane (Luke 22:43):** In the Garden of Gethsemane, as Jesus prays in agony over the impending crucifixion, an angel from heaven appears to strengthen Him. The angel's presence is supportive, but it is a silent observer of the profound moment of Jesus' submission to God's will.

These instances of angelic observation highlight the reverence and respect with which angels approach significant events. They acknowledge the sanctity of certain moments and serve as a reminder of God's providence and care, even when they do not actively intervene.

## Key Takeaways on the Role of Angels

THE DIVERSE ROLES OF angels in biblical narratives reveal several key takeaways:

1. **Messengers of Divine Revelation:** Angels serve as intermediaries between God and humanity, conveying critical messages, prophecies, and revelations that shape the course of history.
2. **Agents of Divine Intervention:** Angels act as instruments of divine guidance, protection, and deliverance, ensuring the safety and well-being of the faithful.
3. **Witnesses to Divine Events:** Angels witness significant events, affirming the authenticity and importance of these occurrences.
4. **Comforters in Times of Distress:** In moments of distress, angels provide solace and guidance, offering comfort to those facing physical or emotional challenges.
5. **Instruments of Divine Judgment:** While often associated with messages of grace, angels can also serve as instruments of divine judgment, executing God's righteous purposes.
6. **Protectors of the Faithful:** Angels protect the faithful, serving as guardians in times of conflict and uncertainty as this aligns with God's Will.
7. **Role in Worship and Praise:** Angels engage in continuous worship and praise, setting an example for believers in their adoration of God's holiness.
8. **Soldiers in Spiritual Warfare:** Angels participate in spiritual warfare, battling against demonic forces and cosmic adversaries.

9. **The Silent Observers:** In some instances, angels serve as silent observers, acknowledging the sanctity of significant events without active intervention.

The multifaceted roles of angels in biblical narratives enrich our understanding of their significance in the unfolding drama of salvation. They are not mere messengers but active participants in God's divine plan, fulfilling various functions that contribute to the overarching purpose of redemption and the glorification of God.

As we continue our exploration in the subsequent chapters, we will further explore the unseen war between angels and demons and the consequences of this spiritual battle for believers. This deeper understanding will show how the faithful can equip themselves with the "armour of God" to fend off the devil's oppression and his forces.

# Chapter 3: Demons in the Bible

## The Origins of Satan

The origins of Satan are shrouded in mystery, with biblical texts offering glimpses into his enigmatic past. In Ezekiel 28 and Isaiah 14, scholars often interpret passages traditionally associated with earthly kings as allegorical depictions of Satan's fall from grace. In Ezekiel 28:12-17, the prophet addresses the king of Tyre. It describes the king as an "anointed cherub" in the garden of Eden, adorned with precious stones and blameless until iniquity was found in him. Similarly, Isaiah 14:12-15 portrays the king of Babylon as a fallen star, exalting himself above the stars of God and aspiring to ascend to the heights of heaven.

These passages provide symbolic imagery that hints at the pride and rebellion that led to Satan's downfall. According to tradition, Satan was once a high-ranking angel in heaven, endowed with beauty, wisdom, and authority. However, consumed by pride and envy, he sought to exalt himself above God and rebelled against His divine authority. As a result, Satan was cast out of heaven, along with a third of the angels who joined him in his rebellion (Revelation 12:4).

## The Character of Satan

SATAN'S CHARACTER IS multifaceted, embodying various attributes that define his persona as the adversary of God and humanity. Throughout Scripture, Satan is depicted as a cunning deceiver, a relentless accuser, and a malevolent force seeking to undermine God's plan for creation.

1. **Cunning Deceiver:** Satan is often portrayed as the master of deception, using cunning and deceit to lead humanity astray. In the Garden of Eden, Satan appears in the form of a serpent

and deceives Eve by twisting God's words and appealing to her desires (Genesis 3:1-5). This act of deception results in the Fall of humanity, as Adam and Eve disobey God's command and are expelled from the Garden.

2. **Relentless Accuser:** Satan is also known as the accuser of the brethren, constantly seeking to condemn and accuse believers before God. In the book of Job, Satan accuses Job of serving God only for personal gain, challenging his integrity and faithfulness (Job 1:9-11). Similarly, Satan accuses Joshua, the high priest before the angel of the Lord, of seeking to bring condemnation upon him (Zechariah 3:1-2). Satan's accusations aim to undermine believers' confidence in God's forgiveness and redemption, fostering feelings of guilt, shame, and unworthiness.

3. **Malevolent Adversary:** Satan is depicted as the ultimate adversary, waging war against God and humanity. In Revelation 12:9, Satan is described as the great dragon, the ancient serpent, who deceives the whole world. Throughout history, Satan has sought to disrupt God's plan for redemption by tempting, accusing, and dividing humanity. His malevolent actions have led to suffering, sin, and spiritual bondage as he seeks to thwart God's purposes and establish his own dominion over creation.

The character of Satan, as depicted in Scripture, is one of cunning deception, relentless accusation, and malevolent opposition to God and humanity. His origins trace back to a time of prideful rebellion in heaven, where he sought to exalt himself above God and was cast out as a result. Throughout history, Satan has waged war against God's plan for redemption, using deception, accusation, and division to lead humanity astray. However, despite Satan's best efforts, God remains sovereign and victorious, ultimately triumphing over evil through the sacrificial death and resurrection of Jesus Christ.

## Satan's Strategy

IN THE COSMIC BATTLE between good and evil, Satan, the adversary, plays a central role as the chief antagonist. From the Garden of Eden to the Book of Revelation, the Bible provides a rich tapestry of narratives that reveal Satan's relentless efforts to disrupt God's plan for humanity.

At the heart of Satan's rebellion lies his insatiable desire for power and glory. Before his fall from grace, Satan was a high-ranking angel endowed with beauty and wisdom (Ezekiel 28:12-17). However, consumed by pride and jealousy, he sought to exalt himself above God, leading to his expulsion from heaven (Isaiah 14:12-15). This prideful ambition continues to drive Satan's actions as he seeks to establish his own dominion and undermine God's authority.

Satan's hatred for humanity stems from his envy of God's love and affection towards His creation. Unlike angels, humans were created in the image of God and endowed with the capacity for intimate relationships with their Creator (Genesis 1:26-27). Satan's resentment towards humanity is fueled by his jealousy of the special bond shared between God and His people. By tempting Adam and Eve in the Garden of Eden, Satan aimed to sever this relationship and assert his dominance over humanity (Genesis 3:1-6).

### Satan's Tactics

1. **Deception:** Satan is the ultimate deceiver, employing cunning and deceit to lead humanity astray. His first act of deception is seen in the Garden of Eden, where he distorts God's truth and deceives Eve into disobeying God's command (Genesis 3:1-5). Throughout biblical history, Satan continues to sow seeds of doubt and confusion,

masquerading as an angel of light to deceive both individuals and nations (2 Corinthians 11:14). His deceptive tactics often involve twisting God's Word and enticing people with false promises of power, knowledge, and pleasure.

2. **Temptation:** Satan preys on human weaknesses and vulnerabilities, tempting individuals to indulge in sinful desires. In the wilderness, Satan tempts Jesus by appealing to His physical hunger, pride, and ambition (Matthew 4:1-11). Similarly, Satan tempts King David with the lust of the flesh, leading to his adultery with Bathsheba and subsequent downfall (2 Samuel 11:1-5). Satan's strategy of temptation exploits humanity's innate desires for pleasure, success, and self-gratification, enticing them to forsake God's commands in pursuit of fleeting pleasures.

3. **Accusation:** Satan is also known as the accuser of the brethren, constantly seeking to condemn and discourage believers through accusations and condemnation (Revelation 12:10). In the book of Job, Satan accuses Job of serving God only for personal gain, challenging his integrity and faithfulness (Job 1:9-11). Similarly, Satan accuses Joshua, the high priest before the angel of the Lord, of seeking to bring condemnation upon him (Zechariah 3:1-2). Satan's accusations aim to undermine believers' confidence in God's forgiveness and redemption, fostering feelings of guilt, shame, and unworthiness.

4. **Division:** Satan's strategy of division seeks to sow discord and disunity within communities and relationships. Jesus warns of Satan's divisive tactics, declaring that a house divided against itself cannot stand (Mark 3:24-25). Satan instigates division among believers through gossip, slander, and bitterness, leading to strife and conflict within the body of Christ (Ephesians 4:31-32). Satan promotes false teachings

and doctrines that cause division and schisms within the church, leading believers astray from the truth (1 Timothy 4:1-3).

Satan's tactics throughout biblical history reveal a relentless adversary determined to disrupt God's plan for humanity. Driven by pride, envy, and hatred, Satan employs deception, temptation, accusation, and division to undermine God's authority and lead people astray. However, despite Satan's efforts, God remains sovereign and victorious, ultimately triumphing over evil through the sacrificial death and resurrection of Jesus Christ. As believers, we are called to be vigilant and discerning, resisting Satan's schemes through prayer, obedience to God's Word, and reliance on the power of the Holy Spirit. In doing so, we can stand firm in faith, knowing that God has already secured the ultimate victory over the powers of darkness.

## Corrupting the Messianic Bloodline

IN THE DIVINE NARRATIVE of salvation history, the promised Messiah is the culmination of God's redemptive plan for humanity. From the protoevangelium in Genesis to the prophecies of the coming Messiah in the Old Testament, the anticipation of a saviour to redeem mankind from sin and death permeates the biblical narrative. However, Satan, the adversary, recognised the threat posed by the Messiah to his dominion and endeavoured to corrupt the bloodline through which the Messiah would come. This comprehensive exploration aims to explore Satan's tactics in corrupting the messianic bloodline, unravelling his sinister schemes to thwart God's plan of redemption.

### Satan's Recognition of the Messianic Promise

Before delving into Satan's specific tactics, it is essential to understand his awareness of the messianic promise and its significance. From the moment God pronounced judgment upon the serpent in the Garden of Eden, declaring that the seed of the woman would bruise the serpent's head (Genesis 3:15), Satan recognised the threat posed by the promised Messiah. This protoevangelium signalled Satan's eventual defeat and the restoration of humanity's broken relationship with God. Consequently, Satan became determined to subvert God's plan by corrupting the bloodline through which the Messiah would come.

**Satan's Tactics in Corrupting the Messianic Bloodline**

1. **Temptation and Corruption of Humanity:** Satan's first tactic in corrupting the messianic bloodline involved enticing humanity into sin and rebellion against God. In the pre-Flood era, the sons of God (fallen angels) intermingled with human women, resulting in the birth of the Nephilim (Genesis 6:1-4). This unholy union corrupted the human gene pool. Fallen angel influence further caused widespread wickedness and violence on the earth. By polluting the human bloodline, Satan sought to prevent the emergence of a righteous lineage from which the Messiah would descend.

2. **Persecution and Oppression of God's Chosen People:** Throughout Israel's history, Satan instigated persecution and oppression against God's chosen people, aiming to annihilate the line of descendants through which the Messiah would come. For instance, during the time of Pharaoh's rule in Egypt, Satan inspired Pharaoh to issue a decree to kill Hebrew male infants, seeking to eradicate the Israelites (Exodus 1:15-22). Similarly, the massacre of innocent children by King Herod in Bethlehem in response to the birth of Jesus exemplifies Satan's desperate attempt to eliminate the potential Messiah (Matthew 2:16-18).

3. **Spiritual Corruption and Apostasy:** In addition to physical persecution, Satan sought to corrupt God's chosen people spiritually through idolatry, apostasy, and disobedience. The Israelites' propensity to turn away from God and worship

foreign gods resulted in divine judgment and exile (Jeremiah 2:11-13). Satan exploited the weaknesses and vulnerabilities of Israel's leaders, inciting them to forsake their covenant relationship with God and lead the nation into spiritual ruin. By fostering spiritual corruption and apostasy, Satan aimed to thwart the emergence of a righteous lineage from which the Messiah would arise.

4. **Attempts to Sabotage Jesus' Ministry:** As the prophesied Messiah drew near, Satan intensified his efforts to sabotage Jesus' ministry and prevent the fulfilment of God's plan of redemption. In the wilderness, Satan tempted Jesus with offers of power, wealth, and authority, seeking to derail His mission (Matthew 4:1-11). Throughout Jesus' earthly ministry, Satan incited opposition, rejection, and hostility from religious leaders and authorities, culminating in His crucifixion on the cross (John 8:44; Luke 22:3; Matthew 27:22-25). However, unbeknownst to Satan, Jesus' sacrificial death would ultimately secure victory over sin and death, fulfilling the messianic promise and providing salvation for humanity.

Satan's tactics in corrupting the messianic bloodline reveal a relentless adversary determined to thwart God's plan of redemption. From the corruption of humanity before the Flood to the persecution of God's chosen people and the attempts to sabotage Jesus' ministry, Satan employed various strategies to hinder the emergence of the promised Messiah. However, despite Satan's relentless efforts, God remained faithful to His covenant promises, ensuring that the Messiah would ultimately triumph over sin and death. As believers, we are called to remain vigilant against Satan's schemes, standing firm in faith and trusting in the sovereignty of God's providence.

## Major Satanic Interventions

HERE ARE SOME INSTANCES where Satan attempted to disrupt God's plan throughout biblical history:

**Temptation of Eve:**

IN THE GARDEN OF EDEN, Satan tempted Eve to eat from the forbidden tree, leading to the Fall of humanity (Genesis 3:1-6).

The temptation of Eve in the Garden of Eden is a pivotal event in biblical history, serving as the catalyst for the Fall of humanity and the introduction of sin into the world. This narrative, found in Genesis 3:1-6, offers profound insights into Satan's tactics, human vulnerability, and the consequences of disobedience.

The setting of the temptation is the idyllic Garden of Eden, where God placed Adam and Eve and entrusted them with dominion over creation. In this paradise, they enjoyed intimate fellowship with God. They could eat from any tree except the Tree of the Knowledge of Good and Evil. However, Satan, disguised as a serpent, enters the scene and engages Eve in conversation.

Satan's approach is subtle yet cunning. He begins by casting doubt on God's command, asking Eve, "Did God really say, 'You must not eat from any tree in the garden?'" (Genesis 3:1). By questioning the veracity of God's word, Satan seeks to undermine Eve's confidence in God's authority and wisdom. Eve responds by affirming God's command but adds that they are not even to touch the forbidden fruit, which God did not originally stipulate (Genesis 3:2-3). This slight deviation from God's instruction reveals Eve's vulnerability to deception and manipulation.

Satan then proceeds to directly contradict God's command, asserting that eating the forbidden fruit will not lead to death but will instead open their eyes and make them like God, knowing good and evil (Genesis 3:4-5). Here, Satan appeals to Eve's desire for knowledge, wisdom, and autonomy, enticing her with the promise of becoming like God. This appeal to pride and self-interest proves effective. Eve is drawn to gaining knowledge and wisdom beyond what God has ordained.

Eve succumbs to Satan's deception and temptation, as she "saw that the fruit of the tree was good for food and pleasing to the eye, and also desirable for gaining wisdom" (Genesis 3:6). She takes the fruit, eats it, and shares it with Adam, who also partakes. In this act of disobedience, Adam and Eve defy God's command, severing their intimate relationship with Him and ushering in the consequences of sin for themselves and all of humanity.

The temptation of Eve offers profound insights into Satan's tactics and human vulnerability to deception. Satan's strategy involves questioning God's word, distorting truth, appealing to human desires, and sowing seeds of doubt and disobedience. Eve's response highlights the danger of yielding to temptation and the devastating consequences of sin. However, amidst the darkness of disobedience, the promise of redemption and restoration shines brightly, foreshadowing God's plan to reconcile humanity to Himself through the sacrifice of Jesus Christ.

**Consequences of Sin:** As depicted in the aftermath of Adam and Eve's disobedience in the Garden of Eden, the consequences of sin reverberate throughout biblical history and have profound implications for humanity. Genesis 3:7-24 vividly illustrates the far-reaching effects of sin, encompassing spiritual, relational, and physical dimensions.

1. **Spiritual Consequences:** The immediate consequence of Adam and Eve's sin is their awareness of their nakedness and their attempt to cover themselves with fig leaves (Genesis 3:7). This newfound shame and guilt signify a rupture in their relationship with God as they seek to hide from His presence. Sin separates humanity from God, disrupting the intimacy and fellowship that once characterised their

relationship. The spiritual consequence of sin is alienation from God, resulting in spiritual death and separation from His presence (Isaiah 59:2).

2. **Relational Consequences:** Sin affects humanity's relationship with God and distorts individual relationships. In Genesis 3:12-13, Adam blames Eve for his disobedience, while Eve blames the serpent. This pattern of blame-shifting and brokenness foreshadows the fracturing of human relationships due to sin. Throughout Scripture, we see the devastating effects of sin on families, communities, and nations, as pride, jealousy, selfishness, and conflict tear apart the fabric of society. Sin breeds division, strife, and discord, undermining the harmony and unity that God intended for His creation.

3. **Physical Consequences:** In addition to spiritual and relational consequences, sin brings about physical suffering and death. God pronounces curses upon Adam, Eve, and the serpent, introducing pain, toil, and mortality into the world (Genesis 3:16-19). Eve is destined to experience pain in childbirth, while Adam is condemned to labour and sweat for his sustenance. Humanity's mortality is underscored by the expulsion from the Garden of Eden and the denial of access to the Tree of Life, symbolising eternal separation from God's presence (Genesis 3:22-24).

4. **Cosmic Consequences:** The consequences of sin extend beyond the individual and interpersonal realms to impact the entire created order. Paul writes in Romans 8:20-22 that creation was subjected to futility and decay due to human sin, groaning in anticipation of redemption. The natural world bears the scars of sin, manifesting in disease, disasters, and ecological degradation. Sin's distortion of God's original design disrupts the harmony and balance of the created order,

leading to suffering and destruction.

Despite the devastating consequences of sin, the narrative of Genesis 3 also contains the promise of redemption and restoration. God's pronouncement of judgment on the serpent includes the prophecy of the offspring of the woman who will crush the serpent's head (Genesis 3:15), foreshadowing the coming of Jesus Christ, the ultimate conqueror of sin and death. Through His sacrificial death and resurrection, Jesus offers forgiveness, reconciliation, and new life to all who believe, reversing the effects of sin and restoring humanity's relationship with God. Thus, while the consequences of sin are dire, the hope of salvation through Christ provides a glimmer of light amidst the darkness of sin's aftermath.

## Cain's Jealousy and Murder of Abel:

*SATAN EXPLOITED CAIN'S jealousy towards his brother Abel, leading to the first murder (Genesis 4:1-8).*

Revealing the ongoing battle between good and evil, righteousness and sin. This narrative serves as a microcosm of the broader spiritual conflict between God's kingdom and the forces of darkness.

At its core, the story of Cain and Abel highlights the consequences of sin and the destructive influence of jealousy, anger, and pride. Cain's jealousy towards his brother Abel stems from God accepting Abel's offering while rejecting his own. This jealousy festers into anger and resentment, ultimately leading Cain to commit the heinous act of murder.

Cain's jealousy and subsequent actions can be seen as manifestations of the enemy's tactics to sow discord, division, and destruction among God's people. Satan, the adversary, seeks to exploit human weaknesses and vulnerabilities, using jealousy, anger, and pride as weapons to undermine God's purposes and disrupt His plan for humanity.

Cain's murder of Abel represents the tragic consequences of sin and the victory of evil in the lives of individuals who yield to its influence. Sin not only separates humanity from God but also fractures relationships and leads to violence and death. In this sense, Cain becomes a pawn in the enemy's hands, succumbing to the temptation to commit the ultimate act of rebellion against God by taking his brother's life.

However, God's justice and mercy shine brightly amidst the darkness of Cain's sin. God confronts Cain about his sin and warns him of the consequences, allowing him to repent and turn from his wickedness. This demonstrates God's desire for reconciliation and restoration, even in the face of humanity's rebellion.

The account of Cain and Abel foreshadows the ultimate victory of righteousness over sin through the promised seed of the woman who will crush the serpent's head (Genesis 3:15). This seed ultimately finds fulfilment in Jesus Christ, who triumphs over sin and death through His sacrificial death and resurrection. In Christ, believers find forgiveness, redemption, and victory over the forces of darkness.

The account of Cain and Abel highlights the ongoing battle between good and evil, righteousness and sin. It emphasises the enemy's tactics to exploit human weaknesses and vulnerabilities, leading to discord, division, and destruction. Yet, amidst the darkness, God's justice and mercy prevail, offering hope and redemption to all who turn to Him in faith.

**Human-created Religion:** Viewing Cain's actions sheds light on the early development of religious practices and beliefs in human history. Cain's account provides insights into how humans sought to connect with the divine and make sense of their existence through their own designed religious rituals and offerings.

In the narrative, Cain and Abel bring offerings to the Lord, reflecting their desire to worship and honour God. As a farmer, Cain presents an offering of the fruit of the ground, while Abel, as a shepherd, offers the firstborn of his flock. The differing nature of their offerings suggests distinct approaches to religious worship and expression.

Cain's offering of the fruit of the ground may symbolise his reliance on his efforts and achievements. As a farmer, Cain may have viewed his offering as representing his labour and productivity, seeking to earn God's favour through his works. This perspective aligns with the concept of a human-made religion centred on self-sufficiency and merit-based acceptance by the divine.

On the other hand, Abel's offering of the firstborn of his flock reflects a different mindset. As a shepherd, Abel may have understood the significance of sacrifice and dependence on God's provision. His offering of the firstborn emphasises trust in God's providence and recognition of His sovereignty over all creation. This perspective aligns more closely with a faith-based religion centred on humility, obedience, and trust in God's grace.

Cain's reaction to God's acceptance of Abel's offering and rejection of his own reveals the underlying motivations and attitudes behind his religious practices. Instead of humbly accepting God's judgment and seeking to understand His reasons, Cain becomes angry and resentful. His response suggests a sense of entitlement and self-righteousness, indicative of a human-made religion focused on outward appearances and personal gain.

Cain's subsequent actions, culminating in the murder of his brother Abel, emphasise the dangers of pride, jealousy, and misplaced religious zeal. Cain's misguided religious beliefs and practices lead to tragic consequences, resulting in the first act of fratricide in human history.

Cain's account highlights the complexities of religious expression and belief systems in early human civilisation. It illustrates how religious practices can be influenced by human ego, pride, and self-interest, leading to both sincere worship and misguided devotion. Ultimately, Cain's example is a cautionary tale about humility, faith, and a genuine relationship with the divine in all religious pursuits.

**Corruption Before the Flood:**

*SATAN INFLUENCED HUMANITY to become corrupt and wicked, leading to God's decision to send the Flood (Genesis 6:5-8).*

The account of the corruption before the flood sheds light on the spiritual dimensions of human sin and the ongoing conflict between the forces of darkness and the kingdom of God.

1. **Influence of Dark Forces:** From a spiritual warfare perspective, the corruption before the Flood can be seen as the result of demonic influence and spiritual oppression. The sons of God intermarrying with the daughters of men may represent a form of spiritual corruption, where fallen angels or demonic entities exert influence over humanity, leading to moral and spiritual decay. This interpretation aligns with New Testament teachings on spiritual forces of darkness and their role in deceiving and tempting humanity (Ephesians 6:12).

2. **Struggle for Dominion:** The corruption before the Flood can also be viewed as a manifestation of the ongoing struggle for dominion between the kingdom of God and the kingdom of darkness. Satan, the adversary, seeks to establish his own dominion over creation and thwart God's purposes by corrupting humanity and leading it into sin. The proliferation of wickedness and violence before the Flood may be seen as part of Satan's attempt to undermine God's plan for humanity and disrupt the establishment of His kingdom on

earth.

3. **Spiritual Oppression and Bondage:** The corruption before the Flood highlights the reality of spiritual oppression and bondage experienced by humanity as a result of sin. The pervasive wickedness and violence described in Genesis 6 reveal the depth of human depravity and the enslaving power of sin. From a spiritual warfare perspective, this bondage may be understood as the result of spiritual strongholds and demonic influence, which hold individuals and societies captive to sin and disobedience.

4. **Divine Judgment and Deliverance:** The narrative of the Flood also emphasises the theme of divine judgment and deliverance in the context of spiritual warfare. God's decision to judge the earth and destroy all living creatures reflects His commitment to righteousness and justice in the face of human rebellion and wickedness. Yet, amidst the judgment, God provides a means of deliverance for the righteous through the ark, preserving a remnant of humanity and signalling His faithfulness to His covenant promises.

5. **Hope for Redemption:** Despite the devastation of the Flood, the corruption before it serves as a precursor to God's plan of redemption and restoration. Through the lineage of Noah, God continues His redemptive purposes, ultimately culminating in the coming of Jesus Christ, who defeats the powers of darkness and offers salvation to all who believe. From a spiritual warfare perspective, the corruption before the Flood serves as a reminder of the ongoing battle between good and evil while pointing towards the hope of ultimate victory and restoration in Christ.

Understanding the corruption before the Flood provides valuable insights into the cosmic dimensions of human sin and God's redemptive purposes. It emphasises the reality of spiritual oppression, the struggle for dominion between the kingdom of God and the kingdom of darkness, and the hope of redemption through Jesus Christ. As we engage in spiritual warfare, may we stand firm in the faith, trusting in God's power to overcome the forces of darkness and bring about His kingdom on earth.

**Tower of Babel:**

*SATAN INSTIGATED REBELLION against God by influencing people to build the Tower of Babel, resulting in the dispersion of languages and nations (Genesis 11:1-9).*

The Tower of Babel narrative represents human pride, rebellion, and the influence of spiritual forces seeking to thwart God's purposes and establish their dominion.

1. **Symbolism of the Tower:** From a spiritual warfare perspective, the Tower of Babel can be seen as more than just a physical structure. It symbolises humanity's collective rebellion against God's authority and its attempt to ascend to divine status. The tower represents the pinnacle of human achievement and ambition, fueled by the desire for self-glorification and autonomy. In this interpretation, the tower becomes a focal point of spiritual warfare, drawing the attention of both heavenly and demonic forces.

2. **Influence of Spiritual Forces:** Behind the scenes of human ambition and pride, spiritual forces are at work, manipulating and deceiving humanity to fulfil their own agendas. Satan, as the archenemy of God, seeks to thwart God's plan for humanity by fostering rebellion and discord. The Tower of Babel incident serves as a manifestation of Satan's influence, as he exploits human pride and ambition to incite rebellion

against God. Demonic forces may have influenced the minds and hearts of the people, fueling their desire to build the tower and defy God's commands.

3. **Division and Confusion:** The confusion of languages and the scattering of humanity at Babel are not merely natural consequences of human pride but are orchestrated by spiritual forces seeking to sow discord and division. By confounding their language, God disrupts their unity and cooperation, thwarting their plans for self-glorification. From a spiritual warfare perspective, this act of division serves to weaken the forces of evil and hinder their ability to exert control over humanity.

4. **God's Sovereignty and Victory:** Despite the rebellion at Babel and the influence of spiritual forces, God remains sovereign and in control. His intervention demonstrates His power and authority over creation, foiling the enemy's plans and asserting His divine purposes. The scattering of humanity ultimately serves God's redemptive plan as He continues to work through individuals and nations to fulfil His promises. From a spiritual warfare perspective, the Tower of Babel incident emphasises the ongoing battle between good and evil, with God ultimately emerging victorious.

## Michael the Archangel and Satan Engage in a Battle

*THE CONFRONTATION BETWEEN Michael the archangel and Satan, as described in the Book of Jude, provides profound insights into the nature of spiritual warfare and the cosmic conflict between the forces of good and evil (Jude 1:9).*

The confrontation between Michael and Satan is mentioned in the context of Jude's warning against false teachers and their destructive influence within the church. Jude compares these false teachers to rebellious angels who have rejected their proper authority and indulged in sinful behaviour. In verse 9, Jude provides an intriguing parallel by referencing an incident involving Michael, the archangel and Satan over the body of Moses.

While the details of this confrontation are not elaborated upon in the Bible, it is clear that Michael and Satan engage in a significant spiritual battle. The fact that Michael, an archangel of high rank and authority in the heavenly realms, contends with Satan emphasises the seriousness of the conflict. It suggests that even celestial beings are not immune to the influence of evil and must actively engage in spiritual warfare to combat it.

The confrontation between Michael and Satan highlights several key principles:

1. **The Reality of Spiritual Warfare**: The passage reaffirms the reality of spiritual warfare—a cosmic struggle between the forces of good and evil. This battle extends beyond the physical realm and involves celestial beings with spiritual powers and principalities.

2. **The Authority of God's Servants**: Michael's role as an archangel demonstrates the authority and power granted to God's servants in the spiritual realm. Despite Satan's attempts to assert his dominance, Michael confronts him with divine authority and resolves to resist his influence.

3. **The Importance of Spiritual Discernment**: The confrontation between Michael and Satan emphasises the importance of spiritual discernment in recognizing and resisting the schemes of the enemy. Believers are called to be vigilant and discerning, equipped with the armour of God to stand firm against the devil's tactics (Ephesians 6:10-18).

4. **The Victory of God's Kingdom**: Ultimately, the confrontation between Michael and Satan points to the

ultimate victory of God's kingdom over the forces of darkness. While spiritual battles may rage on, the final outcome is assured through the triumph of Jesus Christ, who disarmed the powers and authorities and made a public spectacle of them, triumphing over them by the cross (Colossians 2:15).

The confrontation between Michael and Satan, as described in the Book of Jude, is a powerful reminder of the reality of spiritual warfare and the ongoing cosmic conflict between good and evil. It emphasises the authority of God's servants, the importance of spiritual discernment, and the ultimate victory of God's kingdom over the forces of darkness. As believers, we are called to stand firm in faith, knowing that the battle belongs to the Lord and that He has already secured the victory through His Son, Jesus Christ.

The conflict over Moses' body likely stemmed from Satan's desire to exploit Moses' legacy and influence for his own purposes, possibly by inciting people to worship Moses rather than God. This addition enhances our understanding of the spiritual dynamics in the confrontation between Michael and Satan described in the Book of Jude.

Satan, known for his cunning and deceptive tactics, may have sought to pervert the reverence due to Moses, a revered figure in Jewish tradition, by manipulating his burial site or inciting disputes over his remains. By fostering idolatry or false worship centred on Moses, Satan could undermine the true worship of God and divert attention away from the Lord's sovereignty and authority.

In engaging in this conflict, Michael the archangel is a defender of God's truth and a protector of His people, resisting Satan's attempts to distort the proper worship and reverence due to God alone. The confrontation over Moses' body thus becomes a battle for control over earthly relics and a symbolic struggle for the purity of worship and the sanctity of God's name.

This interpretation aligns with the broader themes of spiritual warfare and the clash between truth and deception woven throughout Scripture. It emphasises the importance of discerning and resisting the subtle schemes of the enemy, who seeks to distort and pervert the worship of God and lead people astray from the path of righteousness.

The conflict over Moses' body serves as a poignant reminder of the ongoing spiritual battle for the hearts and minds of humanity—a battle in which believers are called to stand firm in the faith, equipped with the armour of God, and empowered by the Holy Spirit to resist the wiles of the devil and uphold the truth of God's Word.

**Pharaoh's Decree to Kill Hebrew Infants:**

*SATAN INFLUENCED PHARAOH to issue a decree to kill Hebrew male infants, attempting to thwart God's plan to deliver the Israelites from slavery (Exodus 1:15-22).*

Examining Pharaoh's decree of infanticide reveals the underlying spiritual conflict between God's redemptive plan and the forces of evil. This narrative, found in Exodus 1:8-22, showcases how earthly rulers can become pawns in the enemy's schemes to thwart God's purposes and oppress His people.

The account unfolds against the backdrop of Egypt, where the Israelites have become numerous and powerful people. Fearing the growth of the Israelites, Pharaoh, driven by a spirit of fear, envy, and oppression, issues a decree to kill all Hebrew male infants at birth. This decree reflects Pharaoh's attempt to exert control, suppress the Israelites, and prevent the fulfilment of God's promise to bless and multiply Abraham's descendants.

Pharaoh's decree represents an act of spiritual oppression and resistance against God's covenant people. Pharaoh, influenced by demonic forces, becomes a willing instrument in Satan's attempt to hinder God's redemptive plan. His actions align with the enemy's strategy to instil fear, sow division, and destroy the future leaders of Israel.

Pharaoh's decree echoes the broader spiritual conflict between God and the powers of darkness. Throughout Scripture, we see instances of earthly rulers being influenced or possessed by demonic forces to oppose God's purposes (e.g., King Herod's attempt to kill the infant Jesus in Matthew 2:16). These rulers serve as agents of spiritual oppression, seeking to suppress the spread of God's kingdom and silence His people.

However, God's sovereignty and providence shine brightly amidst the darkness of Pharaoh's decree. He raises up courageous individuals, such as the Hebrew midwives Shiphrah and Puah, who defy Pharaoh's orders and refuse to carry out infanticide. Their civil disobedience demonstrates their faithfulness to God and commitment to protecting innocent lives.

God intervenes on behalf of His people, thwarting Pharaoh's plans and preserving the life of Moses, who will play a pivotal role in leading the Israelites out of bondage. Through divine providence, Moses is rescued from the Nile River by Pharaoh's daughter and raised in the royal court, where he receives the education and training necessary to fulfil his calling as the deliverer of God's people.

Pharaoh's decree of infanticide illuminates the ongoing conflict between God's redemptive purposes and the forces of evil. Pharaoh, influenced by demonic forces, becomes a willing instrument in Satan's attempt to hinder God's plan for His people. However, God's sovereignty, providence, and faithfulness prevail as He raises courageous individuals and intervenes on behalf of His chosen ones. This narrative serves as a reminder of the spiritual warfare surrounding us and the importance of remaining steadfast in faith, trusting in God's ultimate victory over the powers of darkness.

**Temptation of Jesus:**

*SATAN TEMPTED JESUS in the wilderness, trying to derail His mission by offering worldly power and authority (Matthew 4:1-11).*

The temptation of Jesus unveils a profound understanding of the cosmic battle between good and evil, righteousness and sin. This pivotal event, recorded in the Gospels of Matthew, Mark, and Luke, showcases the confrontation between Jesus, the Son of God, and Satan, the adversary.

The setting of the temptation is significant, as it occurs immediately after Jesus' baptism in the Jordan River, where the Holy Spirit descends upon Him like a dove. The voice of God declares, "This is my beloved Son, with whom I am well pleased" (Matthew 3:17). Jesus, filled with the Holy Spirit, is led by the Spirit into the wilderness to be tempted by the devil.

The wilderness symbolises a place of spiritual testing and preparation, reminiscent of the Israelites' forty years of wandering in the desert and the prophet Elijah's testing time in the wilderness. Jesus' forty days of fasting and prayer prepare Him for the spiritual battle ahead.

Satan, recognising Jesus' vulnerable state after forty days of fasting, seizes the opportunity to tempt Him. The temptations presented by Satan are strategic and multifaceted, targeting Jesus' identity, mission, and relationship with God.

Firstly, Satan tempts Jesus to satisfy His physical hunger by turning stones into bread. This temptation challenges Jesus' identity as the Son of God and His dependence on the Father for sustenance. However, Jesus responds by affirming His trust in God's provision and reliance on His Word.

Secondly, Satan tempts Jesus to test God's protection by throwing Himself off the pinnacle of the temple, quoting Scripture to support his suggestion. This temptation challenges Jesus' mission to trust God's timing and ways rather than seeking to manipulate or coerce God into action. Yet again, Jesus responds by quoting Scripture, emphasising the importance of trusting God's Word and refusing to put Him to the test.

Finally, Satan offers Jesus all the kingdoms of the world in exchange for His worship, appealing to Jesus' desire to establish His kingdom on earth. This temptation challenges Jesus' allegiance to God and His commitment to the divine plan of redemption. However, Jesus rejects Satan's offer decisively, affirming His exclusive devotion to God and His kingdom.

The temptation of Jesus represents a pivotal moment in the spiritual warfare between Jesus and Satan. It showcases Jesus' victory over temptation and His unwavering commitment to righteousness and obedience to God's will. Through His triumph over temptation, Jesus demonstrates His authority over the powers of darkness and establishes Himself as the ultimate conqueror of sin and evil.

The temptation of Jesus foreshadows His ultimate victory on the cross, where He defeats sin and death through His sacrificial death and resurrection. As believers, we are called to follow Jesus' example, resist temptation, and stand firm in faith amidst the trials and tribulations of life. In doing so, we participate in the ongoing spiritual warfare against the forces of evil, trusting in God's power and provision to sustain us and lead us to victory.


**Peter's Rebuke of Jesus:**


*SATAN USED PETER TO dissuade Jesus from His sacrificial mission, prompting Jesus to rebuke him (Matthew 16:21-23).*

Peter's rebuke and Jesus' response reveal profound insights into the ongoing battle between God's kingdom, the forces of darkness, and the nature of spiritual authority and discipleship.

Peter's rebuke occurs in Matthew 16:21-23, immediately after Jesus predicts His impending suffering, death, and resurrection. Peter, deeply troubled by Jesus' words, takes Him aside and rebukes Him, saying, "Never, Lord! This shall never happen to you!" (Matthew 16:22). Peter's reaction reflects his sincere devotion to Jesus and his desires to protect Him from harm. However, Jesus responds with a stern rebuke, saying, "Get behind me, Satan! You are a stumbling block to me; you do not have in mind the concerns of God, but merely human concerns" (Matthew 16:23).

Peter's rebuke highlights the tension between God's divine plan and human understanding. Like many of Jesus' disciples, Peter struggles to grasp the significance of Jesus' mission and the necessity of His sacrificial death. His reaction is influenced by worldly thinking and human concerns rather than spiritual discernment and alignment with God's purposes.

Jesus' response to Peter's rebuke is striking and reveals the spiritual battle. By addressing Peter as "Satan," Jesus exposes the underlying spiritual influence behind Peter's words. Satan, the adversary, seeks to oppose God's plan of redemption and deter Jesus from fulfilling His mission. Peter unwittingly becomes a tool of Satan in this moment, as his well-intentioned but misguided words align with the enemy's efforts to hinder Jesus' obedience to the Father's will.

Jesus' rebuke emphasises the importance of spiritual discernment and obedience to God's will. Jesus recognises the spiritual warfare behind Peter's words and confronts it head-on, reaffirming His commitment to fulfil His divine mission, even in the face of opposition. He emphasises the necessity of aligning one's mind with the concerns of God rather than human concerns driven by fear, doubt, or worldly wisdom.

This passage also highlights the nature of spiritual authority and discipleship in God's kingdom. Jesus entrusts Peter, yet He does not hesitate to rebuke Peter when his words oppose God's will. This illustrates the importance of humility, teachability, and submission to God's authority, even for those in positions of leadership and influence.

Peter's rebuke and Jesus' response from a spiritual warfare perspective emphasise the ongoing battle between God's kingdom and the forces of darkness. They highlight the importance of spiritual discernment, obedience to God's will, and humility in discipleship. Ultimately, this passage serves as a reminder of the spiritual realities surrounding us and the necessity of remaining steadfast in faith, aligned with God's purposes, even in the face of opposition and misunderstanding.

**Opposition to Paul's Ministry:**

*SATAN OPPOSED PAUL'S efforts to spread the Gospel, hindering his missionary journeys and inciting persecution (2 Corinthians 11:23-27).*

Exploring the opposition to Paul's ministry provides valuable insights into believers' challenges in God's work and the enemy's tactics to hinder the gospel's spread.

Paul encounters various forms of opposition throughout his ministry, from human adversaries and spiritual forces. These obstacles manifest the broader spiritual conflict between God's kingdom and the forces of darkness.

One aspect of opposition to Paul's ministry is the persecution he faces from unbelieving Jews and Gentiles alike. Paul experiences physical attacks, imprisonment, and slander as he boldly proclaims the gospel and establishes Christian communities. These persecutions reflect the enemy's attempt to silence God's messengers and intimidate believers into abandoning their faith.

Paul encounters spiritual opposition from demonic forces that seek to hinder his ministry and undermine the effectiveness of the gospel message. In his letter to the Ephesians, Paul writes, "For our struggle is not against flesh and blood, but against the rulers, against the authorities, against the powers of this dark world and against the spiritual forces of evil in the heavenly realms" (Ephesians 6:12). This passage highlights the spiritual nature of the warfare in which Paul is engaged and emphasises the need for spiritual discernment and reliance on God's strength.

The tactics employed by the enemy to oppose Paul's ministry include deception, division, and false teaching. In Galatians, Paul warns against false teachers who seek to distort the gospel and lead believers astray (Galatians 1:6-9). These false teachings undermine the authority of Scripture, promote legalism, and compromise the purity of the gospel message. They serve as a tool of the enemy to sow confusion, doubt, and division within the body of Christ.

Despite facing formidable opposition, Paul remains steadfast in his commitment to advancing God's kingdom and fulfilling his calling as an apostle to the Gentiles. He relies on the power of the Holy Spirit, fellow believers' support, and God's armour to withstand the enemy's attacks and continue preaching the gospel with boldness and perseverance.

The opposition to Paul's ministry from a spiritual warfare perspective emphasises the reality of the ongoing battle between God's kingdom and the forces of darkness. It highlights the various forms of opposition faced by believers engaged in God's work and the tactics employed by the enemy to hinder the gospel's spread. Ultimately, Paul's example inspires believers to stand firm in their faith, rely on God's strength, and engage in spiritual warfare with courage and perseverance.

**False Teachers in the Early Church:**

*SATAN INFILTRATED THE early Christian community with false teachers and doctrines, leading to divisions and confusion (2 Corinthians 11:13-15).*

Examining false teachers and doctrines unveils the pervasive influence of deception and distortion in spiritual beliefs and practices.

Throughout history, false teachers have emerged, promoting doctrines that deviate from the truth of God's Word and lead people astray from the path of righteousness.

False teachers and doctrines can be understood as manifestations of the enemy's strategy to undermine God's truth and disrupt His plan of redemption. Satan, the adversary, seeks to deceive and confuse people by distorting the truth and leading them away from God's Word. False teachers become willing instruments in Satan's hands, propagating lies and falsehoods that appeal to human desires and lead to spiritual bondage and destruction.

The New Testament contains numerous warnings about false teachers and doctrines. Jesus Himself warns of false prophets who will come in sheep's clothing but inwardly are ravenous wolves, seeking to deceive and mislead God's people (Matthew 7:15). The apostles Paul, Peter, and John also address the dangers of false teaching and urge believers to be vigilant and discerning (2 Corinthians 11:13-15; 2 Peter 2:1-3; 1 John 4:1).

False teachers often promote doctrines that deny essential truths of the Christian faith, such as the deity of Christ, the atonement, salvation by grace through faith, and the authority of Scripture. They may distort biblical teachings, add to or subtract from the gospel message, or promote their agendas and ideologies. Their teachings appeal to human pride, greed, and lust, offering promises of prosperity, success, and spiritual enlightenment apart from genuine repentance and faith in Christ.

False teachers often infiltrate the church, posing as leaders and shepherds of God's flock. They exploit their positions of authority to exert control, manipulate others, and exploit vulnerable believers for personal gain. Their influence can lead to division, strife, and spiritual bondage within the body of Christ, hindering its effectiveness in advancing God's kingdom.

Combatting false teachers and doctrines requires discernment, vigilance, and adherence to the truth of God's Word. Believers are called to test the spirits, hold fast to sound doctrine, and expose falsehoods with the light of God's truth (1 Thessalonians 5:21; Ephesians 5:11). They are to be like the Bereans, who examined the Scriptures daily to see if what was being taught aligned with God's Word (Acts 17:11).

The battle against false teachers and doctrines is part of the broader spiritual warfare between God's kingdom and the forces of darkness. Believers must stand firm in the truth, equipped with the armour of God, and empowered by the Holy Spirit to resist deception and advance the cause of Christ in a world filled with spiritual deception and falsehood.

**Persecution of the Righteous:**

*SATAN INCITED PERSECUTION against Christians throughout history, aiming to suppress the spread of the Gospel and undermine faith (1 Peter 5:8).*

The account of Job provides profound insights into the nature of suffering, the character of God, and the unseen battle between good and evil. The Book of Job presents a narrative of a righteous man who undergoes immense suffering and trials yet remains faithful to God amidst his afflictions.

The account of Job serves as a vivid illustration of the conflict between God and Satan, the accuser. Satan challenges the integrity of Job's faith, suggesting that Job's righteousness is merely a result of God's blessings and protection. Satan accuses Job of serving God only for personal gain and predicts that Job will curse God if his blessings are taken away (Job 1:9-11).

God allows Satan to test Job's faith but sets limits on the extent of the trials Job will endure (Job 1:12; 2:6). As a result, Job experiences a series of devastating losses, including the death of his children, the destruction of his property, and the onset of a painful and debilitating illness. Despite his suffering, Job refuses to curse God and maintains his trust in Him, declaring, "Though he slay me, yet will I hope in him" (Job 13:15).

The attacks on Job reveal several important truths:

1. **The Reality of Spiritual Attacks**: Job's suffering is not merely a result of natural disasters or random occurrences but is orchestrated by Satan as part of a larger spiritual battle. This highlights the reality of spiritual attacks against the righteous, as Satan seeks to undermine their faith and allegiance to God.

2. **The Sovereignty of God**: Despite Job being allowed to undergo trials and suffering, God remains sovereign over all creation. He sets limits on the extent of Satan's power. He ultimately uses Job's suffering to restore Job and vindicate his righteousness.

3. **The Integrity of the Righteous**: Job's response to suffering demonstrates the integrity and steadfastness of the righteous in the face of adversity. Despite his losses and pain, Job refuses to abandon his faith or blame God for his circumstances. Instead, he wrestles with questions of suffering and ultimately submits to God's wisdom and sovereignty.

4. **The Importance of Trusting God**: Job's story emphasises trusting God in suffering and trials. Despite not understanding the reasons for his suffering, Job trusts God's goodness and faithfulness. His example challenges believers to trust God's character, even when circumstances seem bleak and incomprehensible.

5. **The Victory of Faith**: Ultimately, Job's story ends in victory as God restores and blesses him abundantly (Job 42:10-17).

Job's faithfulness in suffering serves as a testimony to God's faithfulness and vindicates the righteousness of the upright.

The Job narrative illuminates the unseen battle between God and Satan, the reality of spiritual attacks against the righteous, and the importance of trusting God amidst suffering and trials. Job's example inspires believers to remain steadfast in faith, knowing that God is sovereign over all things and will ultimately bring about victory and redemption.

Further, considering the persecution of believers unveils the deeper dimensions of the ongoing battle between God's kingdom and the forces of darkness. Persecution, throughout history and across cultures, has been a hallmark of the Christian experience, reflecting the spiritual conflict between the values of God's kingdom and the principles of the world.

Persecution can be understood as an attack on the body of Christ orchestrated by the enemy, Satan, and his agents. The apostle Paul describes the struggle against spiritual forces of evil in heavenly realms. He encourages believers to put on the full armour of God to withstand the schemes of the devil (Ephesians 6:10-12). Persecution is one of the primary tactics employed by the enemy to intimidate, silence, and eradicate the witness of believers.

Persecution takes various forms, including physical violence, imprisonment, social ostracism, economic discrimination, and legal harassment. Throughout history, countless believers have suffered and died for their faith, enduring unspeakable hardships and persecution for their allegiance to Christ. The persecution of believers manifests the broader spiritual conflict between light and darkness, truth and lies, righteousness and evil.

Persecution serves to refine and strengthen the faith of believers, purifying them like gold in the fire (1 Peter 1:6-7). It exposes the depth of one's commitment to Christ. It separates genuine disciples from those who profess faith for personal gain or convenience. Persecution also serves as a testimony to the gospel's transformative power, as believers endure suffering with grace, forgiveness, and unwavering faith.

Persecution fulfils Jesus' warning that His followers will face opposition and hatred from the world because they are not of the world (John 15:18-19). The world's hostility towards believers reflects its alignment with the values and priorities of the kingdom of darkness, which opposes the truth of God's Word and seeks to suppress the spread of the gospel.

Despite the hardships and suffering associated with persecution, believers are encouraged to rejoice in their sufferings, knowing that they share in the sufferings of Christ and will also share in His glory (Romans 8:17; 1 Peter 4:13). Persecution is not a sign of defeat but rather a confirmation of one's identity as a follower of Christ and a participant in the spiritual warfare against the powers of darkness.

Persecution highlights persecution as a manifestation of the broader conflict between God's universal kingdom and the forces of darkness. Persecution exposes the spiritual realities behind earthly opposition to the gospel. It serves to refine and strengthen the faith of believers. Ultimately, believers are called to stand firm in the face of persecution, trusting God's sovereignty and remaining faithful.

**Spiritual Warfare:**

*SATAN ENGAGES IN ONGOING spiritual warfare against believers, seeking to deceive, tempt, and discourage them from following God faithfully (Ephesians 6:10-18).*

Recognising spiritual warfare is essential for believers to navigate the unseen battles that rage around them. Spiritual warfare encompasses the ongoing conflict between the kingdom of God and the kingdom of darkness, where believers engage in a spiritual struggle against demonic forces, evil influences, and worldly powers.

Recognising spiritual warfare involves several key elements:

1.  **Understanding the Nature of the Conflict**: Spiritual warfare begins with understanding the nature of the conflict. It is a battle not against flesh and blood but against spiritual forces of evil in the heavenly realms (Ephesians 6:12). Believers are engaged in a cosmic struggle between light and darkness, truth and deception, righteousness and evil.

2.  **Discerning Spiritual Realities**: Recognising spiritual warfare requires recognising spiritual realities beyond the physical realm. It involves seeing beyond the surface level of events and circumstances to discern the underlying spiritual forces at work. This discernment enables believers to identify demonic influences, spiritual strongholds, and manifestations of evil in their lives and communities.

3.  **Being Aware of Spiritual Attacks**: Spiritual warfare involves awareness of spiritual attacks aimed at undermining one's faith, distorting truth, and hindering spiritual growth. These attacks can take various forms, including temptations, doubts, fears, discouragement, and opposition from the enemy. Recognising spiritual attacks enables believers to respond with faith, prayer, and spiritual weapons.

4.  **Engaging in Prayer and Spiritual Warfare**: Recognising spiritual warfare necessitates engaging in prayer and spiritual warfare strategies. Believers are called to put on the full armour of God, including the belt of truth, the breastplate of righteousness, the shoes of the gospel of peace, the shield of faith, the helmet of salvation, and the sword of the Spirit (Ephesians 6:13-17). Prayer is a powerful weapon in spiritual warfare, enabling believers to stand firm against the devil's

schemes and advance the kingdom of God.

5. **Walking in Authority**: Recognising spiritual warfare involves walking in the authority that believers have been given in Christ. Jesus has given believers authority to trample on snakes and scorpions and to overcome all the power of the enemy (Luke 10:19). By exercising this authority in Jesus' name, believers can confront spiritual forces, break strongholds, and bring freedom and deliverance to those oppressed by the enemy.

6. **Staying Rooted in God's Word**: Recognising spiritual warfare requires staying rooted in God's Word. The Bible is the sword of the Spirit, the primary weapon for combating spiritual attacks and discerning truth from lies (Ephesians 6:17). By meditating on Scripture, believers can recognise and resist the enemy's schemes and stand firm in the face of spiritual opposition.

Recognising spiritual warfare involves understanding the nature of the conflict, discerning spiritual realities, being aware of spiritual attacks, engaging in prayer and spiritual warfare, walking in authority, and staying rooted in God's Word. By embracing these principles, believers can effectively navigate the unseen battles that rage around them and experience victory in Christ.

**End-Time Deception:**

*SATAN WILL ORCHESTRATE deception and false miracles during the end times, attempting to lead people astray before the return of Christ (Matthew 24:24).*

Examining end-time deception provides crucial insights into the escalating spiritual conflict as the culmination of history approaches. The Bible warns believers about the rise of deception and falsehood in the last days, signalling the intensification of spiritual warfare and the enemy's desperate attempts to deceive and derail God's people.

End-time deception encompasses various forms of spiritual falsehoods, distortions, and counterfeit manifestations to lead people astray from the truth of God's Word and the reality of His kingdom. The book of Revelation and other prophetic passages in Scripture outlines the emergence of false prophets, false christs, and deceptive signs and wonders in the end times, orchestrated by the enemy to deceive even the elect if possible (Matthew 24:24).

End-time deception operates on multiple levels, targeting individuals, churches, and nations with seductive lies and deceptive schemes. It exploits human vulnerabilities, including pride, greed, fear, and spiritual ignorance, to lure people away from the path of righteousness and into spiritual bondage. False doctrines, cults, and religious movements proliferate, offering counterfeit versions of truth and salvation apart from Jesus Christ.

End-time deception extends beyond religious spheres to encompass political, social, and cultural realms. The rise of secular humanism, moral relativism, and globalism reflects the enemy's strategy to undermine biblical values, erode moral foundations, and promote a godless worldview that rejects the authority of God and His Word. The proliferation of false ideologies, conspiracy theories, and misinformation further contributes to the confusion and deception prevalent in the end times.

End-time deception also includes the emergence of false signs and wonders, supernatural phenomena, and paranormal experiences designed to deceive and manipulate people's spiritual perceptions. The enemy mimics the work of the Holy Spirit, leading people to follow after false prophets and messiahs who perform signs and wonders to deceive the unwary (Matthew 24:24; Mark 13:22).

Recognising end-time deception requires discernment, wisdom, and spiritual vigilance. Believers are called to test the spirits, hold fast to the truth of God's Word, and remain anchored in their relationship with Jesus Christ (1 John 4:1; Ephesians 4:14). They must be on guard against false teachings, deceptive spirits, and seductive lies that seek to undermine their faith and lead them astray.

Believers are called to proactively expose deception, confront falsehood, and share the gospel of truth with others. They are to stand firm in their faith, equipped with the armour of God and empowered by the Holy Spirit, to withstand the enemy's deceptive schemes and advance the kingdom of God in spiritual warfare (Ephesians 6:10-18).

End-time deception highlights the escalating spiritual conflict as history progresses. Believers must be vigilant, discerning, and steadfast in their faith, recognising the signs of deception and holding fast to the truth of God's Word. By remaining anchored in Christ and empowered by the Holy Spirit, believers can overcome the deceptive schemes of the enemy and emerge victorious in the spiritual battles of the end times.

## Key Takeaways on Unveiling the Adversary

KEY TAKEAWAYS FROM unveiling the adversary include the following:

1. **Understanding Spiritual Warfare**: Spiritual warfare encompasses the ongoing conflict between the kingdom of God and the forces of darkness. It involves battles fought in the spiritual realm, impacting individuals and societies.
2. **Satan's Strategies**: Satan employs various strategies to disrupt God's plan, including deception, temptation, persecution, and the distortion of truth. He seeks to undermine faith, lead people astray, and hinder the advancement of God's kingdom.
3. **Human Agents of Evil**: Throughout history, Satan has worked through human agents to carry out his schemes. From Cain's jealousy leading to Abel's murder to Pharaoh's

decree to kill Hebrew male infants, human actions have been influenced by demonic forces to thwart God's purposes.

4.  **Corruption of the Bloodline**: Satan has consistently sought to corrupt the bloodline through which the Messiah would come, aiming to prevent the fulfilment of God's promise of redemption. This includes attempts to disrupt the lineage of Christ and thwart His birth.

5.  **End-time Deception**: In the last days, there will be a proliferation of deception and falsehood, with false prophets, false christs, and deceptive signs and wonders leading many astray. Believers must be vigilant and discerning, holding fast to the truth of God's Word.

6.  **Victory in Spiritual Warfare**: Despite the reality of spiritual warfare, believers can find assurance in God's sovereignty and the victory secured through Jesus Christ. By standing firm in the faith, equipped with spiritual armour and empowered by the Holy Spirit, believers can overcome the enemy's schemes.

7.  **Balancing Understanding of Evil with Faith**: While exploring the darker aspects of spiritual warfare, it is essential to maintain a strong faith in God's sovereignty and goodness. Balancing the negative exploration of evil with an understanding of God's sovereignty emphasizes the impact of a strong faith on believers engaged in spiritual warfare.

8.  **Role of Prayer and Spiritual Discernment**: Prayer is a powerful weapon in spiritual warfare, enabling believers to seek God's protection, guidance, and strength. Spiritual discernment is also crucial for recognizing and resisting the enemy's schemes.

9.  **Authority in Christ**: Believers possess authority in Christ to confront spiritual attacks, resist the enemy, and advance God's kingdom. By exercising this authority and relying on the power of the Holy Spirit, believers can overcome the

forces of darkness.

10. **Final Victory of God's Kingdom**: Ultimately, the victory belongs to God's kingdom, and His purposes will prevail despite the ongoing spiritual battles. Believers can take comfort in the assurance of God's ultimate triumph and the hope of eternal life in Christ.

These key takeaways provide a comprehensive understanding of spiritual warfare and equip believers to battle with courage, wisdom, and faith. Through prayer, reliance on God's Word, and empowerment by the Holy Spirit, believers can stand firm against the enemy's schemes and experience victory in Christ.

• • • •

THE EXPLORATION OF Satan's tactics, motivations, origins, and character, as depicted in Scripture, unveils a profound understanding of the cosmic battle between good and evil. From his prideful rebellion in heaven to his relentless efforts to disrupt God's plan for humanity, Satan emerges as a cunning adversary, employing deception, temptation, accusation, and division to lead humanity astray. However, amidst the darkness of spiritual warfare, the light of God's sovereignty and victory shines brightly. Through the sacrificial death and resurrection of Jesus Christ, God has triumphed over evil, offering redemption, forgiveness, and hope to all who believe. As believers, we are called to stand firm in faith, resisting Satan's schemes through prayer, obedience to God's Word, and reliance on the power of the Holy Spirit. In doing so, we can confidently navigate the challenges of spiritual warfare, knowing that God's kingdom will ultimately prevail and His purposes will be fulfilled.

# Demonic Influences in the Old Testament

While the Old Testament is replete with stories of angelic encounters and divine interventions, it also contains narratives that depict the influence of demonic forces and spiritual adversaries. In this chapter, we explore instances of demonic influences in the Old Testament, shedding light on the nature of these malevolent beings and their impact on human affairs.

## The Serpent in the Garden of Eden (Genesis 3:1-7)

THE SERPENT'S STORY in the Garden of Eden is one of the earliest instances of a demonic presence in the Bible. While the text refers to the serpent, it is widely understood as a symbol of Satan or a demonic entity.

In this narrative, the serpent approaches Eve and questions God's command not to eat from the tree of the knowledge of good and evil. The serpent deceives Eve, leading her to doubt God's intentions and to partake of the forbidden fruit. Adam, too, succumbs to this temptation. This act of disobedience results in the fall of humanity and introduces sin into the world.

The serpent's role as a deceiver and tempter highlights the presence of a malevolent spiritual force at work in the early days of human history. The consequences of this encounter reverberate throughout the Old and New Testaments, illustrating the enduring impact of demonic influences on the human condition.

## The Story of Job (Job 1:6-12)

THE BOOK OF JOB PROVIDES a striking portrayal of a dialogue between God and a character referred to as "Satan" or "the accuser." This entity questions Job's righteousness and challenges God's protection of him. In this narrative, Satan is not portrayed as an independent adversary but as an accuser in God's heavenly court.

As a result of this dialogue, Job experiences a series of calamities, including losing his wealth, health, and loved ones. While the book does not explicitly describe Satan as a demon, it does paint him as an opponent to God. The character's role in afflicting Job raises questions about the nature of suffering and the involvement of malevolent spiritual forces.

This narrative emphasises the broader theological theme of divine sovereignty and human suffering, where Satan plays a significant role in testing Job's faith.

## The Nephilim (Genesis 6:1-4)

THE ENIGMATIC MENTION of the Nephilim in Genesis 6 has intrigued scholars and readers for centuries. This passage suggests that the "sons of God" intermarried with the "daughters of men," resulting in the birth of the Nephilim. While the "sons of God" identity is debated, some interpretations suggest they were fallen angels or supernatural beings.

The Nephilim are often associated with giants and are seen as the offspring of this union between the "sons of God" and human women. Their presence in the narrative raises questions about the influence of supernatural beings on human affairs.

While the Bible does not provide extensive details about the Nephilim, their presence hints at the blurred boundaries between the human and supernatural realms. The subsequent narrative of the Flood, which follows the account of the Nephilim, reflects divine judgment on the wickedness of humanity and may be seen as a response to the influence of these mysterious beings.

## The Witch of Endor (1 Samuel 28:3-25)

IN THE STORY OF KING Saul and the Witch of Endor, we encounter an example of a human practitioner of the occult who is believed to communicate with the dead. Saul, facing imminent battle and abandoned by God, seeks out the witch to summon the spirit of the deceased prophet Samuel.

The story unfolds with the witch successfully summoning Samuel's spirit, which foretells Saul's impending defeat and death. This narrative is a cautionary tale about the dangers of seeking supernatural knowledge through occult practices.

While the Bible does not explicitly identify the source of the spirit the witch summoned, it highlights the reality of spiritual forces beyond the physical world. It also emphasises the consequences of engaging with such forces without divine guidance.

## Evil Spirits and King Saul (1 Samuel 16:14-23)

KING SAUL'S LIFE IS marked by periods of torment and distress caused by an evil spirit from the Lord. This malevolent spirit troubles Saul, leading to episodes of erratic behaviour and deep emotional distress.

In these passages, the Lord sends an evil spirit as a form of divine judgment upon Saul. To alleviate his suffering, Saul's servants suggest that a skilled musician, David, be brought to play the harp for him. David's music soothes Saul and provides temporary relief from the torment of the evil spirit.

This narrative highlights the biblical recognition of evil spirits as agents of divine judgment. While the text doesn't provide in-depth information about the nature of these spirits, it demonstrates their ability to influence human psychology and behaviour.

## The Story of the Gadarene Demoniac (Mark 5:1-20)

WHILE MOST INSTANCES of demonic influence in the Old Testament are veiled or indirect, the New Testament provides a vivid account of a man possessed by a legion of demons. This story, often called the Gadarene demoniac, is in the Gospel of Mark.

In this narrative, Jesus encounters a man living among the tombs in the region of the Gadarenes. The man is possessed by many demons identified as "Legion." They cause the man to exhibit violent and self-destructive behaviour. When Jesus confronts the demons, they beg Him not to send them out of the region but into a herd of swine. Jesus permits them to enter the swine, who then rush into the sea and perish.

This story is a powerful demonstration of Jesus' authority over demonic forces. It also illustrates the capacity of demons to possess and torment individuals, leading to destructive behaviours.

## Key Takeaways on Demonic Influences in the Old Testament

THE NARRATIVES OF DEMONIC influences in the Old Testament provide several key takeaways:

1. **The Presence of Spiritual Adversaries:** The Bible acknowledges the presence of spiritual adversaries, such as Satan, the accuser, and potentially fallen angels.
2. **Influence on Human Affairs:** These entities can influence human decisions and actions, leading to consequences and suffering.
3. **Blurred Boundaries:** Some narratives, such as the mention of the Nephilim, suggest blurred boundaries between the human and supernatural realms.
4. **Dangers of Occult Practices:** The story of the Witch of Endor warns about the dangers of engaging in occult practices to seek supernatural knowledge.

5. **Divine Authority over Demons:** The story of the Gadarene demoniac illustrates Jesus' authority over demonic forces, offering hope and deliverance to those tormented by such influences.

1. **Divine Judgment and Consequences:** The presence of malevolent forces in the Old Testament narratives often reflects divine judgment or testing, resulting in consequences for individuals or communities.

These Old Testament narratives emphasise the acknowledgement of demonic influences and spiritual adversaries in the biblical text. They serve as cautionary tales, examples of divine judgment, and demonstrations of God's authority over malevolent forces. While the Old Testament provides glimpses into the presence and impact of these entities, it is in the New Testament that the battle between angels and demons and the relevance of the "armour of God" become more prominent, as we will explore in the following chapters.

As we examine the New Testament narratives and the ongoing spiritual warfare between angels and demons, we will gain a deeper understanding of the unseen struggle that continues to shape the lives of believers and the role of the "armour of God" in confronting and overcoming these spiritual challenges.

# Demonic Influences in the New Testament

In the New Testament, the presence and influence of demons become more pronounced, shedding light on the ongoing spiritual battle between good and evil. This chapter explores instances of demonic influences in the New Testament, providing insight into the nature of these malevolent beings and their impact on the lives of believers.

## Demonic Possession and Oppression in the Synoptic Gospels

THE SYNOPTIC GOSPELS (Matthew, Mark, and Luke) provide numerous accounts of Jesus' encounters with individuals who were either demonically possessed or oppressed by evil spirits. These narratives illustrate the reality of spiritual warfare and Jesus' authority over demons.

- **The Man with an Unclean Spirit (Mark 1:21-28):** In the synagogue at Capernaum, Jesus encounters a man with an unclean spirit. The spirit recognises Jesus and cries, "What have you to do with us, Jesus of Nazareth? Have you come to destroy us? I know who you are—the Holy One of God." Jesus rebukes the spirit, and the man is freed from its influence. This episode emphasises Jesus' authority over unclean spirits and their acknowledgement of His divinity.
- **The Gadarene Demoniac (Mark 5:1-20):** The story of the Gadarene demoniac, previously mentioned in the Old Testament section, is also recounted in the New Testament. Jesus delivers the man possessed by a legion of demons, illustrating His power to liberate individuals from extreme oppression.

- **The Boy with an Unclean Spirit (Mark 9:14-29):** A man brings his son, possessed by an unclean spirit, to Jesus' disciples for deliverance. When the disciples are unable to help, the father appeals to Jesus. Jesus rebukes the unclean spirit, which leaves the boy. This narrative demonstrates the complexity of demonic oppression and the necessity of faith in Jesus' authority for deliverance.
- **The Woman with a Spirit of Infirmity (Luke 13:10-17):** In the synagogue, Jesus encounters a woman bent over for eighteen years due to a spirit of infirmity. He declares her free from her affliction, illustrating His power to heal those oppressed by evil spirits.

These accounts in the synoptic Gospels emphasise the reality of demonic possession and oppression during the time of Jesus. They also highlight His authority to deliver individuals from such torment, underscoring the importance of faith in Him.

## The Ministry of Deliverance in the Gospels

IN ADDITION TO INDIVIDUAL encounters, the Gospels record broader instances of Jesus' ministry of deliverance from demonic influences.

- **Casting Out Many Demons (Mark 1:32-34):** The news about Jesus' miraculous powers spreads after healing Simon's mother-in-law. As evening falls, people bring to Him many possessed by demons. He casts out the demons with a word, demonstrating His authority and compassion.
- **The Seventy-Two Sent Out (Luke 10:1-20):** Jesus sends out seventy-two of His disciples to proclaim the kingdom of God and heal the sick. They return joyfully, reporting that even

the demons had submitted to them in His name. Jesus affirms their authority over demons and reminds them of the greater reason for joy—belonging to the kingdom of God.

These passages reveal that Jesus' authority extended to the liberation of many from demonic oppression. They also point to the broader mission of the disciples in continuing His work of deliverance.

## The Binding of the Strong Man (Matthew 12:22-32)

IN THIS IMPORTANT PASSAGE, the Pharisees accuse Jesus of casting out demons by the power of Beelzebul, the prince of demons. Jesus responds with a profound explanation of the spiritual dynamics at play.

He begins by stating that a kingdom divided against itself cannot stand. He asserts that if He casts out demons by the Spirit of God, the kingdom of God has come upon them. He then presents a parable about binding the strong man to plunder his house. This imagery reflects Jesus' authority over demonic forces and His mission to release people from their influence.

The passage ends with a warning about blasphemy against the Holy Spirit, a sin that will not be forgiven. This serves as a sobering reminder of the gravity of rejecting the work of the Holy Spirit, who empowers Jesus' ministry of deliverance from demonic forces.

## The Pigs and the Demon-Possessed Man (Matthew 8:28-34)

IN THIS NARRATIVE, Jesus and His disciples encounter two demon-possessed men in the region of Gadara. Upon recognising Jesus, the demons plead not to be tormented and request to enter a nearby herd of swine. Jesus permits them, and the entire herd rushes into the sea and drowns.

The swineherds' reaction and the city's people is one of fear, and they ask Jesus to leave their region. This event showcases Jesus' authority over demons. Still, it also illustrates the fear and resistance that can arise when confronted with the power of God over evil forces.

## The Daughter of the Syrophoenician Woman (Mark 7:24-30)

IN THIS ACCOUNT, A Syrophoenician woman approaches Jesus, seeking healing for her demon-possessed daughter. Initially, Jesus responds that the children must be fed first, but the woman's persistence leads Him to commend her faith. He then casts the demon out of her daughter from a distance.

This narrative highlights Jesus' authority over demonic forces and the importance of persistent faith in seeking deliverance. The woman's unwavering trust in Jesus results in her daughter's healing.

## The Deliverance of the Demon-Possessed Boy (Mark 9:14-29)

THIS STORY, PREVIOUSLY mentioned in the section on the synoptic Gospels, showcases the disciples' inability to cast out a demon from a boy. When the boy's father brings him to Jesus, the disciples inquire about their failure. Jesus responds by emphasising the role of faith and prayer in overcoming such challenges.

The narrative emphasises the complexity of demonic oppression and the necessity of a deep reliance on God's power through faith and prayer for effective deliverance.

## The Exorcism of Mary Magdalene (Luke 8:1-3)

LUKE'S GOSPEL INTRODUCES Mary Magdalene, a woman from whom Jesus had casted out seven demons. This brief mention illustrates

Jesus' ministry of deliverance and its profound impact on the lives of those liberated from demonic influences.

## The Seven Sons of Sceva (Acts 19:11-20)

THE BOOK OF ACTS PROVIDES a narrative about the seven sons of Sceva, Jewish exorcists who attempted to cast out demons using the name of Jesus without a genuine relationship with Him. Their attempt results in a humiliating encounter with a demon-possessed man, who overpowers them.

This incident emphasises the importance of a personal relationship with Jesus and the need for genuine faith when engaging in spiritual warfare. It also highlights the potential dangers of confronting evil spirits without a true connection to the source of spiritual authority.

## Demonic Influence on the Unbelieving

THE NEW TESTAMENT ALSO highlights the reality of demonic influence on those who do not believe in Christ.

- **The Veil of Unbelief (2 Corinthians 4:3-4):** In his second letter to the Corinthians, the apostle Paul speaks of a "veil" that covers the minds of unbelievers, preventing them from seeing the light of the gospel of the glory of Christ. This spiritual blindness is attributed to the "god of this age," who is understood as a reference to Satan. The passage emphasises the idea that unbelief can be influenced by demonic forces.
- **The Sons of Disobedience (Ephesians 2:1-3):** In Ephesians, Paul speaks of the spiritual condition of unbelievers before they come to faith in Christ. He describes them as being "dead in trespasses and sins" and as following "the prince of the power of the air, the spirit who now works in the sons of disobedience." This suggests that those who do not believe in

Christ are influenced by spiritual forces opposed to God.

These passages illuminate the concept of spiritual warfare in the context of belief and unbelief. They indicate that those who reject Christ may be influenced by malevolent spiritual forces that blind them to the truth.

## Spiritual Warfare and the Armour of God (Ephesians 6:10-18)

IN THE NEW TESTAMENT, the apostle Paul provides essential guidance on the nature of spiritual warfare and the tools available to believers to resist demonic influences. Ephesians 6:10-18 is a foundational passage that addresses the believer's need to be equipped for this unseen battle.

Paul instructs believers to "put on the whole armour of God" to stand against the devil's schemes. This spiritual armour includes:

- The belt of truth
- The breastplate of righteousness
- Shoes of the gospel of peace
- The shield of faith
- The helmet of salvation
- The sword of the Spirit (the Word of God)
- Praying in the Spirit

Each component of the armour is metaphorical, representing virtues and tools that are essential for spiritual warfare. The belt of truth signifies the importance of living in truth and righteousness. The breastplate of righteousness guards the heart and ensures moral purity. The shoes of the gospel of peace reflect the readiness to share the message of Christ. The shield of faith provides protection against the enemy's attacks. The helmet of salvation safeguards the mind with the hope of salvation. The sword of the Spirit, the Word of God, is the offensive weapon for defeating the enemy. Prayer in the Spirit maintains a constant connection with God.

Paul's teaching in Ephesians 6 emphasises the reality of spiritual warfare and the need for believers to actively engage in the battle with the resources provided by God. It highlights the ongoing struggle between angels and demons and the role of believers in this cosmic conflict.

## Key Takeaways on Demonic Influences in the New Testament

THE NARRATIVES AND passages in the New Testament reveal several key takeaways regarding demonic influences:

1. **The Prevalence of Demonic Activity:** The New Testament demonstrates the prevalence of demonic possession and oppression during the time of Jesus and the early church.
2. **Jesus' Authority over Demons:** The Gospels showcase Jesus' authority in delivering individuals from demonic oppression and possession, highlighting His role as the ultimate source of liberation.
3. **The Importance of Faith:** Many narratives stress the importance of faith in Jesus' name for deliverance from demonic influences, emphasising the role of belief in the process of healing and liberation.
4. **The Complex Nature of Spiritual Warfare:** Some stories, like the exorcism of the demon-possessed boy, illustrate the complexity of demonic oppression and the need for deep faith and prayer in confronting it.
5. **The Influence of Demons on Unbelievers:** The New Testament suggests that demons can play a role in blinding the minds of unbelievers, contributing to their unbelief.

6. **The Armour of God:** The apostle Paul's teachings in Ephesians 6 provide a comprehensive framework for understanding spiritual warfare and the essential components of the believer's spiritual armour.

These key takeaways emphasise the reality of spiritual warfare in the New Testament and the significance of believers' active participation in confronting demonic influences. The "armour of God" shows how they can stand firm and resist the devil's schemes.

As we continue exploring the unseen struggle between angels and demons, we will explore deeper into the consequences of this ongoing battle for believers and how they can effectively employ the "armour of God" to fend off the oppression of the devil and his forces.

# The Role of Demons in Biblical Narratives

In the tapestry of biblical narratives, demons play various roles, reflecting their malevolent nature and their impact on human affairs. These narratives provide insights into the characteristics and tactics of these spiritual adversaries and the consequences of their influence on individuals and communities.

## Tempters and Tormentors

DEMONS OFTEN SERVE as tempters and tormentors, seeking to lead individuals astray and cause distress.

- **Temptation of Jesus (Matthew 4:1-11):** In this well-known narrative, Jesus is led into the wilderness to be tempted by the devil. The devil tempts Him with offers of power, authority, and comfort. Jesus resists these temptations by quoting Scripture and reaffirming His commitment to God's will. This episode illustrates the devil's role as a tempter, trying to divert Jesus from His divine mission.
- **The Demoniac at the Synagogue (Mark 1:23-28):** A man with an unclean spirit disrupts a synagogue service, crying out and challenging Jesus. The spirit acknowledges Jesus as the Holy One of God but resists His authority. Jesus commands the spirit to leave, and it departs, leaving the man unharmed. This narrative demonstrates the tormenting influence of unclean spirits and Jesus' power to command them.

## Influence on Mental Health

BIBLICAL NARRATIVES also suggest that demonic influences can impact mental health and well-being.

- **The Gerasene Demoniac (Mark 5:1-20):** The story of the Gerasene demoniac, mentioned previously, presents a man who lived among the tombs, possessed by a legion of demons. The demons tormented him, causing self-destructive behaviour and isolation. After Jesus' intervention, the man is found "in his right mind," illustrating the restoration of mental health and well-being.
- **The Demon-Possessed Boy (Mark 9:14-29):** The boy with a mute and deaf spirit, believed to be demon-possessed, displays severe symptoms that affect his physical and mental health. Jesus' deliverance not only heals the boy physically but also restores his mental faculties, allowing him to speak and hear.

These narratives indicate that demons can contribute to mental and emotional distress, and their expulsion can lead to healing and restoration.

## Manifestations of Supernatural Power

IN SOME BIBLICAL ACCOUNTS, demons manifest supernatural power to create fear and resistance.

- **The Man in the Tombs (Luke 8:26-39):** Jesus encounters a man in the Gerasene region who is possessed by a legion of demons. The demons, upon recognising Jesus, beg Him not to torment them. Jesus commands them to leave the man, and they enter a herd of swine, causing them to rush into the sea. This dramatic event illustrates the supernatural power of demons and the fear they can instil.

## Influence on Society and Culture

DEMONIC INFLUENCES are not limited to individual cases but can extend to societal and cultural contexts.

- **The Demon-Possessed Slave Girl (Acts 16:16-24):** In Philippi, Paul and Silas encounter a slave girl who is possessed by a spirit of divination. She brings profit to her owners through fortune-telling. When she continually cries out about Paul and Silas being "servants of the Most High God," Paul commands the spirit to leave her, depriving her owners of their source of income. This narrative illustrates how demonic influences can intertwine economic and cultural systems.

- **Ephesus and the Burning of Occult Books (Acts 19:11-20):** In Ephesus, extraordinary miracles are performed by the hands of Paul. Many who had practised magic arts brought their books and burned them publicly. This event reveals the pervasive influence of occult practices and their impact on the culture and spiritual climate of the city.

These narratives show that demonic influences can extend beyond individual experiences to impact societies and cultures, influencing economic and religious practices.

## Influence on Worldviews and Belief Systems

IN CERTAIN BIBLICAL accounts, demons are linked to the promotion of false beliefs and worldviews.

- **The Apostle Paul and Idolatry (1 Corinthians 10:19-21):** In his first letter to the Corinthians, Paul warns against idolatry and the dangers of partaking in the table of demons.

He emphasises that idols and sacrifices are connected to demons, and believers cannot participate in both the Lord's table and the table of demons. This teaching reveals how demonic influences can shape false belief systems and practices.

- **False Prophets and Deceptive Spirits (1 Timothy 4:1-3):** In his first letter to Timothy, Paul cautions against false teachings and doctrines of demons. He notes that some will depart from the faith, following deceitful spirits and teachings that forbid marriage and the consumption of certain foods. This passage emphasises the influence of demons on false belief systems and their ability to lead people away from the truth.

These passages highlight the role of demons in promoting false beliefs and practices that can lead individuals away from a genuine relationship with God.

## Conflict with Divine Forces

WHILE DEMONS SEEK TO influence and oppress, they are also in conflict with divine forces, particularly the angels of God.

- **The Prince of the Kingdom of Persia (Daniel 10:12-14):** In the book of Daniel, the angelic messenger sent to Daniel encounters resistance from a "prince of the kingdom of Persia" for twenty-one days until the archangel Michael comes to his aid. This narrative provides insight into the spiritual conflict between angels and demonic forces in the heavenly realms.
- **Michael and the Dragon (Revelation 12:7-9):** The book of Revelation portrays a cosmic battle between Michael and his

angels and the dragon (often identified as Satan) and his angels. This conflict results in the expulsion of the dragon and his forces from heaven. This passage symbolises the ongoing battle between angels and demons on a cosmic scale.

## The Spread of the Gospel and Deliverance

WHILE DEMONS PLAY A malevolent role in many narratives, the gospel of Jesus Christ brings liberation from their influence.

- **Deliverance and the Healing Ministry of Jesus:** Throughout the Gospels, Jesus' ministry is marked by deliverance from demonic influences. As individuals are set free, the gospel's message spreads, leading many to faith in Christ.
- **The Exorcism of the Demon-Possessed Slave Girl (Acts 16:16-24):** In Philippi, after the slave girl is delivered from her spirit of divination, her owners react with anger, leading to the imprisonment of Paul and Silas. This event demonstrates the liberating power of the gospel and its potential to disrupt the systems built on demonic influences.

## Key Takeaways on the Role of Demons in Biblical Narratives

THE BIBLICAL NARRATIVES regarding demons offer several key takeaways:

1. **Tempters and Tormentors:** Demons often serve as tempters, seeking to divert individuals from God's path and as tormentors, causing suffering and distress.
2. **Influence on Mental Health:** Demons can impact an individual's mental and emotional well-being, contributing to

distress and even mental illness. However, the intervention of Jesus and the power of faith can lead to healing and restoration.

1. **Manifestations of Supernatural Power:** Demons possess supernatural abilities that can create fear and astonishment. Their power is often displayed dramatically, illustrating their malevolence and strength.

2. **Influence on Society and Culture:** Demonic influences can extend beyond individual experiences and impact entire societies and cultures. They may become entwined with economic, religious, and cultural systems, sometimes leading to significant social change.

3. **Influence on Worldviews and Belief Systems:** Demons are linked to promoting false beliefs, idolatry, and deceptive teachings. They can lead people away from the truth and foster belief systems that oppose a genuine relationship with God.

4. **Conflict with Divine Forces:** Demons are in conflict with the angels of God, often depicted as opposing forces in the spiritual realm. These battles occur on a cosmic scale and are part of the ongoing struggle between good and evil.

5. **The Spread of the Gospel and Deliverance:** While demons seek to oppress and deceive, the gospel of Jesus Christ offers liberation from their influence. The ministry of Jesus and the proclamation of the gospel bring deliverance and freedom to those under demonic oppression.

These key takeaways collectively reveal the multifaceted role of demons in biblical narratives, illustrating their influence on individuals, societies, and cultures, as well as their ongoing conflict with divine forces. The narratives also emphasise the liberating power of faith in

Jesus and the transformative impact of the gospel in overcoming the influence of demons.

As we explore the unseen struggle between angels and demons, we will examine the consequences of this spiritual battle for believers and how the "armour of God" equips them to confront and resist the oppression of the devil and his malevolent forces.

# Chapter 4: Worship and the Dangers of Angelolatry

# The Biblical Command to Worship God Alone

Central to the Christian faith is the command to worship God alone. This foundational principle, deeply rooted in the Bible, serves as a stark reminder of the dangers of idolatry and the worship of anything other than the one true God. In this chapter, we will explore the biblical command to worship God exclusively, the consequences of failing to do so, and the relevance of this command in the context of the unseen struggle between angels and demons.

## The Shema: Worship the Lord Your God Alone

THE BIBLE'S CALL TO worship God exclusively encapsulates the "Shema," a foundational declaration of faith for the Jewish people. Found in the Old Testament, specifically in the book of Deuteronomy, the Shema is a profound statement that encapsulates the essence of monotheism and devotion to God.

**Deuteronomy 6:4-5:** "Hear, Israel: Yahweh is our God. Yahweh is one. You shall love Yahweh, your God, with all your heart and with all your soul and with all your might."

This declaration, recited by devout Jews throughout their history, reinforces the absolute oneness of God and the command to love Him with every facet of one's being. It reminds us that no other entity, including angels, should be the object of worship and devotion.

## The First Commandment: You Shall Have No Other Gods

THE TEN COMMANDMENTS, given to Moses on Mount Sinai, are a cornerstone of biblical ethics and worship. The first commandment is a clear directive against worshipping any other gods besides the Lord.

**Exodus 20:3:** "You shall have no other gods before me."

This commandment leaves no room for ambiguity. God's people are instructed to worship Him alone, acknowledging His supreme authority and divinity. The consequences of violating this commandment are profound, as idolatry not only diverts worship from God but also opens the door to the influence of malevolent forces, such as demons.

## Idolatry and Its Consequences

THROUGHOUT THE BIBLE, idolatry is portrayed as a grievous sin with severe consequences. When individuals or nations turn to the worship of false gods or idols, they not only forsake the one true God but also invite spiritual corruption and oppression.

**Deuteronomy 7:25-26:** "You shall burn the engraved images of their gods with fire. You shall not covet the silver or the gold that is on them, nor take it for yourself, lest you be snared in it, for it is an abomination to Yahweh your God. You shall not bring an abomination into your house and become a devoted thing like it. You shall utterly detest and abhor it, for it is a devoted thing."

In this passage, God's people are instructed to destroy the idols and images of foreign gods. The reason is clear: these objects are offensive to God and can ensnare and corrupt those possessing them. Idolatry is equated with spiritual entrapment, and its practice is strongly condemned.

**Leviticus 26:1:** "You shall make for yourselves no idols, neither shall you raise up an engraved image or a pillar, neither shall you place any figured stone in your land to bow down to it, for I am Yahweh your God."

The prohibition against making idols and bowing down to them emphasises the absolute requirement to worship the Lord alone. Any deviation from this commandment carries consequences, both spiritual and practical.

# The Consequences of Idolatry in the Bible

THE CONSEQUENCES OF idolatry are vividly portrayed in the Old Testament. When individuals or nations turned to false gods, they often faced divine judgment and the withdrawal of God's protection.

- **The Golden Calf (Exodus 32):** In one of the most famous incidents of idolatry, the Israelites fashioned a golden calf and worshipped it while Moses was on Mount Sinai. God's anger burned against them, and divine judgment followed. Thousands lost their lives as a result of this idolatrous act.

- **The Worship of Baal (1 Kings 18):** The prophet Elijah's confrontation with the prophets of Baal on Mount Carmel vividly demonstrates the consequences of idol worship. After the prophets of Baal failed to call down fire on their sacrifice, Elijah called upon the Lord, and fire consumed his offering, confirming God's supremacy. The prophets of Baal were subsequently executed.

- **Idolatry in Judah and Israel (Various):** Throughout the history of both the Northern Kingdom of Israel and the Southern Kingdom of Judah, idolatry was a persistent problem. Prophets such as Jeremiah and Isaiah warned of the impending judgment due to the worship of foreign gods. Ultimately, both kingdoms faced destruction and exile due to their idolatry.

These narratives illustrate the destructive power of idolatry and the severe judgment it incurs. The worship of idols not only diverts devotion from God but also opens the door to spiritual oppression and conflict with divine forces.

## The Temptation to Worship Angels

WHILE THE BIBLE'S PRIMARY focus is on prohibiting worshipping false gods and idols, it also addresses the issue of worshipping angels. This is significant in the unseen struggle between angels and demons.

**Colossians 2:18:** "Let no one rob you of your prize by a voluntary humility and worshipping of the angels, dwelling in the things which he has not seen, vainly puffed up by his fleshly mind."

The apostle Paul's words in Colossians caution against the veneration of angels. While angels are powerful and glorious beings, they are not to be the object of worship. To do so is to deviate from the command to worship God alone and to potentially open oneself to deception and spiritual danger.

**Revelation 19:10:** "I fell before his feet to worship him. He said to me, 'Look! Don't do it! I am a fellow bondservant with you and your brothers who hold the testimony of Jesus. Worship God, for the testimony of Jesus, is the Spirit of Prophecy.'"

In the book of Revelation, when the apostle John falls at the feet of an angel to worship, the angel's response is clear: worship God, not the angel. This encounter emphasises the unwavering commitment to the exclusive worship of God, even in the presence of mighty and glorious angelic beings.

## The Battle for Worship in the Unseen Struggle

THE BATTLE FOR WORSHIP is a central theme in the unseen struggle between angels and demons. Demons, in their malevolence, seek to divert worship away from God and towards themselves or other false gods. This is often accomplished through deception, temptation, and the promotion of idolatry.

**1 Corinthians 10:20-21:** "But I say that the things which the Gentiles sacrifice, they sacrifice to demons and not to God, and I don't desire that you would have fellowship with demons. You can't both drink the cup of the Lord and the cup of demons. You can't both partake of the table of the Lord and the table of demons."

In his first letter to the Corinthians, the apostle Paul warns against associating with idolatrous practices. He emphasises that when people offer sacrifices to false gods, they are, in fact, engaging with demons. This spiritual reality emphasises the significance of worshipping God alone, as participation in idolatry can lead to communion with demonic forces.

## The Armour of God: Protection in the Unseen Struggle

IN THE CONTEXT OF THE unseen struggle between angels and demons, the "armour of God" takes on profound importance. The command to worship God alone is intrinsically linked to the believer's spiritual armour, essential for resisting the devil's schemes and his forces.

**Ephesians 6:11-12:** "Put on the whole armour of God, that you may be able to stand against the wiles of the devil. For our wrestling is not against flesh and blood, but against the principalities, against the powers, against the world's rulers of the darkness of this age, and against the spiritual forces of wickedness in the heavenly places."

This passage from Ephesians 6 highlights the spiritual warfare that believers are engaged in. The "armour of God" is the protective equipment that enables them to stand against the devil's strategies and the spiritual forces of darkness. This armour includes truth, righteousness, the gospel of peace, faith, salvation, the Word of God, and prayer. Each component plays a vital role in preserving the believer's unwavering commitment to worship God alone and resist the allure of false gods and idols.

## Key Takeaways: The Biblical Command to Worship God Alone

IN SUMMARY, THE BIBLICAL command to worship God alone is a foundational principle in the Christian faith, deeply embedded in the Bible. Key takeaways regarding this command include:

1. **The Shema and Monotheism:** The Shema encapsulates the oneness of God and the command to love Him with all one's heart, soul, and might, reinforcing the belief in monotheism.

2. **The First Commandment:** The first of the Ten Commandments expressly instructs that no other gods should be worshipped besides the Lord, establishing the exclusivity of divine worship.

3. **Idolatry and Its Consequences:** The Bible portrays idolatry as a grave sin with severe consequences, often leading to divine judgment and spiritual corruption.

4. **The Worship of Angels:** The New Testament cautions against the worship of angels, emphasising that worship should be directed exclusively to God.

5. **The Battle for Worship:** The battle for worship is central to the unseen struggle between angels and demons. Demons seek to divert worship away from God through deception and temptation.

6. **The Armour of God:** The "armour of God" is the believer's spiritual protection against the schemes of the devil and his forces, enabling them to resist the allure of false gods and idols.

The command to worship God alone is a guiding principle in the face of the unseen struggle between angels and demons. It emphasises the unwavering commitment to the one true God and the importance of standing firm in the spiritual battle. As we explore the consequences of this battle for believers, we will explore the significance of the "armour of God" and its role in resisting the oppression of the devil and his malevolent forces.

While angels play a significant role in the biblical narrative and Christian theology, worship directed towards these celestial beings is explicitly discouraged in the Bible. This chapter explores the dangers and pitfalls of angel worship, drawing upon relevant biblical references to provide insight into the potential spiritual perils of deviating from the command to worship God alone.

## Angels as Messengers and Servants

IN CHRISTIAN THEOLOGY, angels are commonly understood as heavenly messengers and servants of God. They are portrayed as beings created by God to carry out His divine will and to minister to those on Earth. The Bible consistently emphasises their role as messengers and instruments of God's purpose.

**Hebrews 1:14:** "Aren't they all serving spirits, sent out to do service for the sake of those who will inherit salvation?"

This verse from the book of Hebrews emphasises the servitude of angels and their purpose in serving the needs of humanity. They are not to be objects of worship but rather facilitators of God's will and His relationship with His creation.

## Angels as Witnesses to God's Glory

ANGELS ALSO SERVE AS witnesses to the glory of God. Their presence often heralds significant moments in biblical history, underscoring their role as instruments of divine revelation and proclamation.

**Luke 2:13-14:** "Suddenly, there was with the angel a multitude of the heavenly army praising God, and saying, 'Glory to God in the highest, on earth peace, good will toward men.'"

The angels' appearance to the shepherds at the birth of Jesus is a powerful example of their role in bearing witness to God's glory. They direct the shepherds' attention to God, not to themselves. Their purpose is to declare the good news of Christ's birth and to glorify God.

**Revelation 22:8-9:** "Now I, John, am the one who heard and saw these things. When I heard and saw, I fell down to worship before the feet of the angel who had shown me these things. He said to me, 'See, you don't do it! I am a fellow bondservant with you and with your brothers, the prophets, and with those who keep the words of this book. Worship God.'"

In the book of Revelation, the apostle John's reaction to an angelic messenger is to fall down in worship. However, the angel immediately corrects John, emphasising that they are fellow servants and that worship should be directed exclusively to God. This interaction serves as a clear admonition against angel worship.

## The Danger of Diverting Worship from God

THE BIBLE WARNS AGAINST diverting worship from God to any created being, including angels. The consequences of such diversion are severe, as it not only violates the command to worship God alone but also opens the door to spiritual deception and danger.

**Exodus 20:3-5:** "You shall have no other gods before me. You shall not make for yourselves an idol, nor any image of anything that is in the heavens above, or that is in the earth beneath, or that is in the water under the earth: you shall not bow yourself down to them, nor serve them, for I, Yahweh your God, am a jealous God."

The first two of the Ten Commandments explicitly address the worship of other gods and the creation of idols. The consequences of such actions are expressed in the phrase "I am a jealous God," indicating God's exclusivity in deserving worship and His aversion to sharing it with any other entity.

**1 Corinthians 10:14:** "Therefore, my beloved, flee from idolatry."

The apostle Paul's straightforward exhortation to the Corinthians emphasises the importance of avoiding idolatry, including worshipping beings other than God.

## The Allure of Angel Worship

WHILE THE BIBLE FIRMLY discourages angel worship, history reveals that this temptation has not been absent from the Christian tradition. The allure of angelic beings, often associated with beauty, power, and supernatural encounters, has led some individuals and groups to veer from the command to worship God alone.

**Colossians 2:18:** "Let no one rob you of your prize by a voluntary humility and worshipping of the angels, dwelling in the things which he has not seen, vainly puffed up by his fleshly mind."

In this Colossian verse, Paul warns against those who might try to lead believers astray through angel worship. The allure of angelic encounters or revelations can lead some to consider venerating them. However, Paul's admonition is clear: do not be deceived or led astray by such practices.

**The Early Church and Angelology:** Some sects and groups developed elaborate angelologies and angel worship in the early Christian centuries. These movements often combined elements of Christianity with angelic veneration, potentially diverting believers' devotion from God to these celestial beings.

## The Deceptive Nature of Angel Worship

ONE OF THE DANGERS of angel worship is its potential for deception. The Bible warns that false teachings and deceptive practices can lead believers away from the truth and into spiritual error.

**1 Timothy 4:1:** "But the Spirit says expressly that in later times some will fall away from the faith, paying attention to seducing spirits and doctrines of demons."

This passage from 1 Timothy highlights the existence of "seducing spirits" and "doctrines of demons" that can lead people away from the true faith. While the specific nature of these seductions is not detailed, it emphasises the potential for deceptive practices that divert worship from God.

**2 Corinthians 11:14-15:** "And no wonder, for even Satan masquerades as an angel of light. Therefore, it is no great thing if his servants also masquerade as servants of righteousness, whose end will be according to their works."

The apostle Paul's warning in 2 Corinthians emphasises the deceptive nature of Satan and his servants. They can masquerade as beings of light, including angels, leading people into error and deception. The consequences of falling for such deception are severe, as they ultimately lead people away from God.

## The Unseen Struggle: Angel Worship and the Armour of God

IN THE CONTEXT OF THE unseen struggle between angels and demons, the issue of angel worship has profound implications. Angel worship not only diverts worship from God but also exposes believers to deceptive spiritual influences.

**Ephesians 6:12:** "For our wrestling is not against flesh and blood, but against the principalities, against the powers, against the world's rulers of the darkness of this age, and against the spiritual forces of wickedness in the heavenly places."

This verse from Ephesians 6 reminds believers that their struggle is not against flesh and blood but against spiritual forces of wickedness in heavenly places. Suppose they allow themselves to be drawn into angel worship. In that case, they risk being ensnared by forces opposing God's purpose.

## The Armour of God and Protection from Deception

THE "ARMOUR OF GOD" is crucial for safeguarding believers from the pitfalls of angel worship and the deceptive strategies of the enemy. Each component of this spiritual armour plays a vital role in resisting the allure of worshipping angels and the associated spiritual dangers.

**Ephesians 6:14-18:** "Stand therefore, having the utility belt of truth buckled around your waist, and having put on the breastplate of righteousness, and having fitted your feet with the preparation of the Good News of peace; above all, taking up the shield of faith, with which you will be able to quench all the fiery darts of the evil one. And take the helmet of salvation, and the sword of the Spirit, which is the word of God; with all prayer and requests, praying at all times in the Spirit, and being watchful to this end in all perseverance and requests for all the saints."

The "armour of God" components include truth, righteousness, the gospel of peace, faith, salvation, the Word of God, and prayer. These elements are essential for protection against deception and the allure of angel worship. Truth keeps believers grounded in God's Word, righteousness guards their hearts, faith shields them from doubt, and the Word of God is a sword of discernment. Prayer connects them to the source of their strength, God Himself.

## Key Takeaways: The Pitfalls of Angel Worship

IN SUMMARY, THE PITFALLS of angel worship are significant and carry potential spiritual dangers:

1. **Angels as Messengers and Servants:** Angels are created beings who serve as messengers and servants of God, not objects of worship.
2. **Angels as Witnesses to God's Glory:** Angels bear witness to God's glory and are not to be the focus of worship.
3. **The Danger of Diverting Worship from God:** Diverting

worship from God to any created being, including angels, is prohibited and carries severe consequences.

4.  **The Allure of Angel Worship:** The allure of angelic beings, with their beauty and power, has historically tempted some individuals and groups to veer from the command to worship God alone.

5.  **The Deceptive Nature of Angel Worship:** Angel worship can be deceptive, leading believers away from the truth and exposing them to spiritual error.

6.  **The Armour of God and Protection from Deception:** The "armour of God" provides the necessary protection against the allure of angel worship and the deceptive strategies of the enemy.

The Bible's clear stance on angel worship emphasises the importance of unwavering devotion to God alone. In the unseen struggle between angels and demons, this commitment becomes a shield against the pitfalls of deviating from the command to worship the one true God. As we explore the consequences of this unseen battle for believers, we will explore the significance of the "armour of God" and its role in resisting the oppression of the devil and his malevolent forces.

# The Consequences of Misplaced Devotion

In the context of the unseen struggle between angels and demons, the consequences of misplaced devotion are profound and far-reaching. This chapter explores the biblical portrayal of the outcomes of worshipping entities other than God, including angels, and the spiritual perils that follow such deviance.

## The Violation of the First Commandment

THE FOUNDATIONAL PRINCIPLE of the command to worship God alone is enshrined in the First Commandment of the Decalogue. Violating this commandment has severe implications not only for individual believers but also for societies and cultures.

**Exodus 20:3:** "You shall have no other gods before me."

When individuals or nations place entities, including angels, before God, they transgress this commandment, with consequences that reverberate throughout their spiritual and moral landscape.

## Divine Jealousy and Wrath

THE BIBLE PORTRAYS God as a jealous deity when it comes to the devotion of His people. The violation of the exclusive worship of God invokes divine anger and judgment.

**Exodus 20:5:** "You shall not bow yourself down to them, nor serve them, for I, Yahweh your God, am a jealous God."

The expression of God's jealousy in this verse signifies His exclusive right to the worship and devotion of His people. To divert this devotion to angels or other beings is to kindle divine wrath.

**Deuteronomy 6:15:** "For Yahweh your God in the midst of you is a jealous God; lest the anger of Yahweh your God be kindled against you, and he destroys you from off the face of the earth."

This verse from Deuteronomy emphasises the gravity of provoking God's jealousy. The consequence of kindling His anger is nothing less than destruction.

## The Corruption of the Heart

MISPLACED DEVOTION, including worshipping angels, corrupts the human heart and leads individuals away from righteousness.

**Jeremiah 17:9:** "The heart is deceitful above all things and exceedingly corrupt. Who can know it?"

The prophet Jeremiah's assessment of the human heart highlights its inherent deceitfulness and susceptibility to corruption. When individuals turn their devotion away from God, their hearts become entangled in spiritual deception and moral decay.

**1 Corinthians 8:4-7:** "Therefore concerning the eating of things sacrificed to idols, we know that no idol is anything in the world and that there is no other God but one. For though there are things that are called 'gods,' whether in the heavens or on earth, as there are many 'gods' and many 'lords,' yet to us there is one God, the Father, of whom are all things, and we for him; and one Lord, Jesus Christ, through whom are all things, and we live through him."

In this passage from 1 Corinthians, the apostle Paul addresses the issue of eating food sacrificed to idols, a practice closely tied to idolatry. He emphasises that there is only one true God. Deviating from this monotheistic devotion leads to confusion and a divided heart.

## Spiritual Bondage and Oppression

MISPLACED DEVOTION, especially when directed towards entities other than God, can lead to spiritual bondage and oppression. The Bible portrays the consequences of idolatry and the worship of false gods as entrapment.

**Psalm 106:36:** "They served their idols, which became a snare to them."

This verse from Psalm 106 describes how the worship of idols became a snare, or a trap, for those who engaged in such practices. Instead of experiencing freedom and liberation, they found themselves in spiritual bondage.

**1 Corinthians 10:20:** "But I say that the things which the Gentiles sacrifice, they sacrifice to demons and not to God, and I don't desire that you would have fellowship with demons."

The apostle Paul's warning in 1 Corinthians 10:20 emphasises the dangerous spiritual reality that accompanies the worship of entities other than God. He links idolatry to fellowship with demons, indicating that such worship opens the door to oppressive spiritual forces.

## Deception and False Teaching

MISPLACED DEVOTION, including the veneration of angels, often leads to deception and false teaching. The allure of angelic encounters can draw individuals into theological error and spiritual delusion.

**1 Timothy 4:1-2 (WEB):** "But the Spirit says expressly that in later times some will fall away from the faith, paying attention to seducing spirits and doctrines of demons, through the hypocrisy of men who speak lies, branded in their own conscience as with a hot iron."

This passage from 1 Timothy warns of those who will fall away from the faith, lured by seducing spirits and doctrines of demons. Such individuals become purveyors of false teaching, leading others into spiritual error.

**2 Corinthians 11:13-15:** "For such men are false apostles, deceitful workers, masquerading as Christ's apostles. And no wonder, for even Satan masquerades as an angel of light. Therefore, it is no great thing if his servants also masquerade as servants of righteousness, whose end will be according to their works."

The apostle Paul's description of false apostles who masquerade as servants of righteousness illustrates the deceptive nature of such individuals and their false teachings. Just as Satan can appear as an angel of light, those who lead others into misplaced devotion can present themselves as bearers of truth.

## Loss of Divine Protection

WHEN INDIVIDUALS DIVERT their worship from God, they risk losing divine protection and guidance. The Bible portrays the consequences of forsaking God in favour of other entities.

**Judges 10:13-14:** "Yet you have forsaken me, and served other gods. Therefore, I will save you no more. Go and cry to the gods which you have chosen. Let them save you in the time of your distress."

This passage from the book of Judges illustrates the divine response to the Israelites' worship of other gods. God declares that He will no longer save them, instructing them to turn to the gods they have chosen. The consequence of misplaced devotion is a forfeiture of divine protection.

## The Assurance of Divine Restoration

WHILE THE CONSEQUENCES of misplaced devotion are grave, the Bible also offers the hope of divine restoration and forgiveness for those who turn back to God with a repentant heart.

**2 Chronicles 7:14:** "If my people, who are called by my name, will humble themselves and pray, and seek my face, and turn from their wicked ways, then I will hear from heaven, and will forgive their sin, and will heal their land."

This verse from 2 Chronicles promises restoration and healing from God. It emphasises the importance of humility, repentance, and a return to the worship of God alone.

## Key Takeaways: The Consequences of Misplaced

## Devotion

IN SUMMARY, THE CONSEQUENCES of misplaced devotion are significant and multifaceted, encompassing divine judgment, spiritual decay, and moral corruption. Key takeaways regarding the consequences of misplaced devotion include:

1. **Violation of the First Commandment:** Worship directed towards entities other than God violates the foundational commandment to worship God alone.
2. **Divine Jealousy and Wrath:** God's jealousy for the devotion of His people is invoked when worship is diverted to other beings, leading to His wrath and judgment.
3. **Corruption of the Heart:** Misplaced devotion corrupts the human heart, leading individuals away from righteousness and truth.
4. **Spiritual Bondage and Oppression:** Worship of entities other than God can result in spiritual bondage and oppression, becoming a snare for those who engage in such practices.
5. **Deception and False Teaching:** Misplaced devotion often leads to deception and false teaching, as individuals are drawn into theological error and spiritual delusion.
6. **Loss of Divine Protection:** Diverting worship from God can result in losing divine protection and guidance, leaving individuals vulnerable to spiritual dangers.
7. **Assurance of Divine Restoration:** The Bible offers hope and the promise of divine restoration and forgiveness for those who turn back to God with a repentant heart.

The consequences of misplaced devotion serve as a solemn warning in the context of the unseen struggle between angels and demons. They emphasise the significance of unwavering commitment to worship God alone and the need to resist the allure of false gods and idols. As we explore the implications of this unseen battle for believers, we will explore the significance of the "armour of God" and its role in safeguarding against spiritual perils.

# Chapter 5: The Unseen Struggle

138

# The Cosmic Battle Between Angels and Demons

The cosmic battle between angels and demons is a central theme in Christian theology. While this battle is often unseen, its implications are profound. In this chapter, we will explore the biblical portrayal of this cosmic struggle, its origins, and its impact on the spiritual realm and the lives of believers.

## The Origin of the Cosmic Battle

WE MUST FIRST EXPLORE its origins to understand the cosmic battle between angels and demons. The Bible provides insights into the rebellion of certain angels and their transformation into demons.

**Isaiah 14:12-15:** "How you have fallen from heaven, morning star, son of the dawn! How you are cut down to the ground, who laid the nations low! You said in your heart, 'I will ascend into heaven! I will exalt my throne above the stars of God! I will sit on the mountain of assembly in the far north! I will ascend above the heights of the clouds! I will make myself like the Most High.' Yet you shall be brought down to Sheol, to the depths of the pit."

These verses from the book of Isaiah offer a glimpse into the fall of Lucifer, often identified as a cherub or angelic being who sought to exalt himself above God. His rebellion led to his expulsion from heaven and his transformation into Satan, the chief of the demons.

**Revelation 12:7-9:** "There was war in the sky. Michael and his angels made war on the dragon. The dragon and his angels made war, but they didn't prevail. There was no place found for them in heaven any more. The great dragon was thrown down, the old serpent, called the devil and Satan, the deceiver of the whole world. He was thrown down to the earth, and his angels were thrown down with him."

The book of Revelation provides further insight into the cosmic battle, depicting a war in heaven where Michael and his angels fight against the dragon (Satan) and his angels. This war results in the expulsion of the rebellious angels from heaven to the earthly realm.

## The Spiritual Realms

THE COSMIC BATTLE OCCURS within the spiritual realms, often concealed from human perception. These realms are essential to understanding the ongoing conflict between angels and demons.

**Ephesians 6:12:** "For our wrestling is not against flesh and blood, but against the principalities, against the powers, against the world's rulers of the darkness of this age, and against the spiritual forces of wickedness in the heavenly places."

Ephesians 6:12 sheds light on the nature of the conflict, indicating that it is not a physical battle but a spiritual one. The battleground is described as the "heavenly places," signifying the spiritual dimensions where this cosmic struggle unfolds.

**Daniel 10:12-13:** "Then he said to me, 'Don't be afraid, Daniel; for from the first day that you set your heart to understand, and to humble yourself before your God, your words were heard. I have come because of your words. But the prince of the kingdom of Persia withstood me twenty-one days; but, behold, Michael, one of the chief princes, came to help me, and I remained there with the kings of Persia.'"

The book of Daniel offers a glimpse into the spiritual realms as it describes a supernatural encounter. In this passage, a heavenly being is delayed by the "prince of the kingdom of Persia" before being aided by Michael, one of the chief princes. This narrative emphasises the complexity of the spiritual dimensions and the battles that occur within them.

## The Role of Angels in the Cosmic Battle

ANGELS ARE DEPICTED as key participants in the cosmic battle, serving as instruments of God's will in opposing the forces of darkness.

**Revelation 12:7:** "There was war in the sky. Michael and his angels made war on the dragon. The dragon and his angels made war."

Revelation 12:7 reveals that Michael and his angels engage in warfare against the dragon (Satan) and his angels. This battle reflects the ongoing struggle between the forces of light and darkness in the spiritual realms.

**2 Kings 6:15-17:** "When the servant of the man of God had risen early, and gone out, behold, an army with horses and chariots was around the city. His servant said to him, 'Alas, my master! What shall we do?' He answered, 'Don't be afraid, for those who are with us are more than those who are with them.' Elisha prayed, saying, 'Yahweh, please open his eyes so he may see.' Yahweh opened the young man's eyes and saw: behold, the mountain was full of horses and chariots of fire around Elisha."

This passage from 2 Kings demonstrates the presence of angelic forces in the earthly realm. Elisha's servant initially perceives only the physical threat of an opposing army. Still, Elisha prays for his eyes to be opened to the spiritual reality. The servant then sees the angelic host surrounding Elisha, ready to defend and protect.

## The Deceptive Strategies of Demons

DEMONS, AS FALLEN ANGELS, are central figures in the cosmic battle. They employ deceptive strategies to oppose God's plan and deceive humanity.

**2 Corinthians 11:14-15:** "And no wonder, even Satan, masquerades as an angel of light. Therefore, it is no great thing if his servants also masquerade as servants of righteousness, whose end will be according to their works."

The apostle Paul's warning in 2 Corinthians 11 highlights the deceptive nature of demons and their leader, Satan. They can masquerade as beings of light and righteousness, leading people into deception and error.

**1 Timothy 4:1:** "But the Spirit says expressly that in later times some will fall away from the faith, paying attention to seducing spirits and doctrines of demons."

This passage from 1 Timothy emphasises the existence of seducing spirits and doctrines of demons that can lead individuals away from true faith. The strategies of demons include false teachings and alluring deceptions.

## The Impact on Believers

THE COSMIC BATTLE BETWEEN angels and demons has a significant impact on the lives of believers. While this battle primarily occurs within the spiritual realms, its consequences are manifested in the earthly realm.

**Ephesians 6:12:** "For our wrestling is not against flesh and blood, but against the principalities, against the powers, against the world's rulers of the darkness of this age, and against the spiritual forces of wickedness in the heavenly places."

Ephesians 6:12 reiterates that believers are engaged in spiritual warfare. The outcome of the cosmic battle affects the earthly realm, and believers are called to stand against the forces of darkness.

**1 Peter 5:8:** "Be sober, be vigilant, because your adversary the devil, as a roaring lion, walks about, seeking whom he may devour."

In 1 Peter 5:8, believers are admonished to be sober and vigilant because the devil, a central figure in the cosmic battle, seeks to devour and destroy. This highlights the very real impact of the spiritual conflict on the lives of individuals.

**Romans 16:20:** "And the God of peace will quickly crush Satan under your feet. The grace of our Lord Jesus Christ is with you."

This verse from Romans conveys the assurance of victory over Satan through the power of God. Believers are not passive observers in the cosmic battle; they have a role in resisting the adversary.

**Colossians 2:15:** "Having stripped the principalities and the powers, he showed them openly, triumphing over them."

Colossians 2:15 highlights the triumphant work of Christ in the cosmic battle. He has disarmed the principalities and powers, publicly displaying His victory over them. Believers are the beneficiaries of this triumph.

## The Role of the "Armour of God"

THE "ARMOUR OF GOD" becomes crucial in the context of the cosmic battle. It equips believers to stand against the devil's wiles and the darkness's spiritual forces.

**Ephesians 6:13:** "Therefore, put on the armour of God, that you may be able to withstand in the evil day, and, having done all, to stand."

Ephesians 6:13 emphasises the importance of putting on the complete "armour of God" to withstand the spiritual challenges that arise in the cosmic battle. This armour serves as how believers can stand firm against the adversary.

**Ephesians 6:14-18:** "Stand therefore, having the utility belt of truth buckled around your waist, and having put on the breastplate of righteousness, and having fitted your feet with the preparation of the Good News of peace; above all, taking up the shield of faith, with which you will be able to quench all the fiery darts of the evil one. And take the helmet of salvation, and the sword of the Spirit, which is the word of God; with all prayer and requests, praying at all times in the Spirit, and being watchful to this end in all perseverance and requests for all the saints."

These verses from Ephesians 6 describe the various components of the "armour of God," including truth, righteousness, the gospel of peace, faith, salvation, the Word of God, and prayer. Each element plays a crucial role in equipping believers for the cosmic battle.

## Key Takeaways: The Cosmic Battle Between Angels and Demons

THE COSMIC BATTLE BETWEEN angels and demons is a central theme in Christian theology. Key takeaways regarding this cosmic struggle include:

1. **The Origin of the Cosmic Battle:** The rebellion of certain angels and their transformation into demons is the origin of the cosmic conflict.
2. **The Spiritual Realms:** The cosmic battle occurs within the spiritual realms, often concealed from human perception.
3. **The Role of Angels in the Cosmic Battle:** Angels are key participants in the battle, serving as instruments of God's will in opposing the forces of darkness.
4. **The Deceptive Strategies of Demons:** Demons employ deceptive strategies to oppose God's plan and deceive humanity.
5. **The Impact on Believers:** The cosmic battle significantly impacts the lives of believers, as they are called to stand against the forces of darkness.
6. **The Role of the "Armour of God":** The "armour of God" equips believers to stand against the devil's wiles and the spiritual forces of darkness.

The cosmic battle between angels and demons emphasises the unseen spiritual realities that shape the world in which believers live. It highlights the importance of spiritual discernment, vigilance, and reliance on the "armour of God" to withstand the adversary and walk in the victory secured by Christ. As we explore the implications of this unseen battle for believers, we will explore the significance of the "armour of God" and its role in safeguarding against spiritual perils.

# How the Spiritual Realm Affects Our World

The spiritual realm, where the cosmic battle between angels and demons unfolds, profoundly impacts the visible world. In this chapter, we will explore how the spiritual realm affects our world, including the lives of believers, the course of human history, and the ultimate destiny of all creation.

## Influence on Human Thoughts and Actions

THE SPIRITUAL REALM significantly influences human thoughts, emotions, and actions. This influence can be subtle and overt, shaping the decisions and behaviours of individuals.

**Ephesians 2:2:** "In which you once walked according to the course of this world, according to the prince of the power of the air, the spirit who now works in the children of disobedience."

Ephesians 2:2 points to the prince of the power of the air, often understood as a reference to Satan, who influences the course of this world. The spirit of disobedience operates within those not aligned with God's truth.

**2 Corinthians 4:4:** "In whom the god of this world has blinded the minds of the unbelieving, that the light of the Good News of the glory of Christ, who is the image of God, should not dawn on them."

The "god of this world," another reference to Satan, is depicted as blinding the minds of unbelievers, preventing them from receiving the light of the Gospel. This spiritual influence hinders individuals from embracing the truth of Christ.

# Influence on Societal Structures and Systems

THE SPIRITUAL REALM also influences societal structures, systems, and cultures. It can be observed in societies' moral and ethical values and their choices collectively.

**Proverbs 14:34:** "Righteousness exalts a nation, but sin is a disgrace to any people."

This verse from Proverbs emphasises the profound impact of righteousness and sin on nations and peoples. The spiritual condition of a society affects its prosperity and honour.

**Psalm 33:12:** "Blessed is the nation whose God is Yahweh, the people whom he has chosen for his own inheritance."

A nation's spiritual foundation, as reflected in its devotion to God, has significant implications for its blessings and divine favour. A nation that acknowledges God is considered blessed.

# Influence on Human Destiny

THE SPIRITUAL REALM not only affects the course of human history but also directly affects the eternal destinies of individuals. It shapes the path to salvation and the ultimate destination of souls.

**John 3:16:** "For God so loved the world, that he gave his one and only Son, that whoever believes in him should not perish, but have eternal life."

John 3:16 encapsulates the pivotal role of the spiritual realm in human destiny. Belief in Christ and acceptance of God's love leads to eternal life, while rejection leads to perishing.

**2 Corinthians 2:15-16:** "For we are a sweet aroma of Christ to God, in those who are saved, and in those who perish; to the one a stench from death to death; to the other a sweet aroma from life to life. Who is sufficient for these things?"

These verses from 2 Corinthians illustrate the contrasting destinies of those who are saved and those who perish. The spiritual realm plays a decisive role in this division as individuals respond to the message of Christ.

## The "Armour of God" as Protection

IN THE SPIRITUAL INFLUENCE on our world, the "armour of God" is the divine protection and defence for believers.

**Ephesians 6:11:** "Put on the whole armour of God, that you may be able to stand against the wiles of the devil."

Ephesians 6:11 emphasises the purpose of the "armour of God" – to enable believers to stand against the deceptive strategies of the devil. This spiritual armour equips them to resist the influences that seek to divert them from God's truth.

**Ephesians 6:14-17:** "Stand therefore, having the utility belt of truth buckled around your waist, and having put on the breastplate of righteousness, and having fitted your feet with the preparation of the Good News of peace; above all, taking up the shield of faith, with which you will be able to quench all the fiery darts of the evil one. And take the helmet of salvation and the sword of the Spirit, which is the word of God."

These verses describe the individual components of the "armour of God," including truth, righteousness, the gospel of peace, faith, salvation, and the Word of God. Each piece is a shield, protection, or weapon to guard against spiritual influences.

## The Role of Prayer

PRAYER, AS A SPIRITUAL discipline, connects believers to the divine realm and strengthens their relationship with God. It is a vital aspect of how the spiritual realm affects our world.

**Ephesians 6:18:** "With all prayer and requests, praying at all times in the Spirit, and being watchful to this end in all perseverance and requests for all the saints."

Ephesians 6:18 emphasises the importance of prayer as part of the "armour of God." It encourages believers to pray at all times in the Spirit, fostering spiritual alertness and perseverance.

**James 5:16:** "Confess your offences to one another, and pray for one another, that you may be healed. The insistent prayer of a righteous person is powerfully effective."

James 5:16 highlights the effectiveness of prayer, especially when offered by the righteous. Prayer can bring about healing and transformation in the lives of individuals and the world.

## Key Takeaways: How the Spiritual Realm Affects Our World

THE SPIRITUAL REALM profoundly impacts our world, influencing human thoughts, societal structures, and individual destinies. Key takeaways regarding how the spiritual realm affects our world include:

1. **Influence on Human Thoughts and Actions:** The spiritual realm exerts a significant influence on human thoughts, emotions, and actions, often shaping decisions and behaviours.

2. **Influence on Societal Structures and Systems:** The spiritual realm influences societal values, moral standards, and cultural norms, affecting the well-being of nations and peoples.

3. **Influence on Human Destiny:** The spiritual realm plays a pivotal role in determining the eternal destinies of individuals, depending on their response to God.

4. **The "Armour of God" as Protection:** The "armour of God" serves as divine protection, enabling believers to stand against the influences of the spiritual realm.

5. **The Role of Prayer:** Prayer connects believers to the divine realm, fostering spiritual growth, healing, and

transformation.

Understanding the profound influence of the spiritual realm on our world is essential for believers as they navigate the unseen struggle between angels and demons. The "armour of God" and the practice of prayer serve as vital tools for resisting negative spiritual influences and aligning with God's truth. The spiritual realm's impact on our world emphasises the importance of spiritual discernment, steadfast faith, and reliance on God's guidance and protection.

• • • •

THE UNSEEN STRUGGLE between angels and demons within the spiritual realm has far-reaching consequences for our visible world. It influences individuals' thoughts, actions, and destinies, shapes societal structures and systems, and emphasises the importance of faith and the "armour of God" as spiritual protection. Believers are called to be vigilant, understand the profound impact of the spiritual realm on our world, and take up the spiritual tools provided by God to stand firm in the face of these influences. As we explore deeper into the implications of this cosmic battle, we will explore the consequences of misplaced devotion, the pitfalls of angel worship, and the importance of worshipping God alone.

# The Believer's Role in the Spiritual War

The cosmic battle between angels and demons is not a conflict from which believers are detached observers. Instead, they play a crucial role in this spiritual war. In this chapter, we will explore the believer's role in the spiritual war, including their responsibilities, the significance of their faith, and their ultimate victory.

## Responsibility of Spiritual Vigilance

BELIEVERS ARE ENTRUSTED with the responsibility of spiritual vigilance. This vigilance involves awareness of the spiritual battle and actively guarding against the enemy's schemes.

**1 Peter 5:8:** "Be sober, be vigilant, because your adversary the devil, as a roaring lion, walks about, seeking whom he may devour."

This verse from 1 Peter 5:8 emphasises the importance of vigilance. Believers must remain sober and watchful because the devil, their adversary, seeks to devour those who are not alert.

**2 Corinthians 2:11:** "That no advantage may be gained over us by Satan; for we are not ignorant of his schemes."

Believers are called not to be ignorant of Satan's schemes. Recognising the enemy's tactics is essential in preventing him from gaining an advantage.

## The Significance of Faith

FAITH IS FUNDAMENTAL to the believer's role in the spiritual war. Through faith, believers overcome the world, resist the enemy, and stand firm in battle.

**1 John 5:4:** "For whatever is born of God overcomes the world. This is the victory that has overcome the world: your faith."

1 John 5:4 highlights the victory that faith brings. Through faith in God, believers can overcome the world and its spiritual challenges.

**Ephesians 6:16:** "Above all, taking up the shield of faith, with which you will be able to quench all the fiery darts of the evil one."

Faith is described as a shield in Ephesians 6:16. This shield of faith is how believers can quench the attacks of the evil one. It is a protective and defensive element of the "armour of God."

## The Believer's Weapons of Warfare

BELIEVERS ARE EQUIPPED with spiritual weapons to battle against spiritual forces. These weapons are not physical but are mighty in God for pulling down strongholds.

**2 Corinthians 10:4:** "For the weapons of our warfare are not of the flesh, but mighty before God to the throwing down of strongholds."

The weapons of the believer's warfare are not physical but spiritual. They are mighty in the sight of God. They are used to dismantle strongholds, places of spiritual resistance and opposition.

**Ephesians 6:17:** "And take the helmet of salvation, and the sword of the Spirit, which is the word of God."

The "sword of the Spirit" is described in Ephesians 6:17 as the Word of God. This weapon is a powerful offensive tool in the believer's spiritual arsenal. It is used to combat spiritual deception and falsehood and discern the heart's thoughts and intents.

## The Power of Prayer

PRAYER IS VITAL TO the believer's role in the spiritual war. It connects them with God, aligns their will with His, and invokes His intervention in the battle.

**Ephesians 6:18:** "With all prayer and requests, praying at all times in the Spirit, and being watchful to this end in all perseverance and requests for all the saints."

In Ephesians 6:18, believers are encouraged to engage in all forms of prayer and pray in the Spirit at all times. This persevering prayer enhances their spiritual awareness and intercedes for fellow believers.

**James 5:16:** "Confess your offences to one another, and pray for one another, that you may be healed. The insistent prayer of a righteous person is powerfully effective."

James 5:16 emphasises the power of prayer offered by righteous individuals. It is described as powerfully effective and is used for healing and transformation.

## Taking Every Thought Captive

THE BATTLEFIELD OF the spiritual war extends to the realm of thoughts and beliefs. Believers are called to take every thought captive to the obedience of Christ.

**2 Corinthians 10:5 (WEB):** "Casting down imaginations and every high thing that is exalted against the knowledge of God, and bringing every thought into captivity to the obedience of Christ."

This verse from 2 Corinthians 10:5 emphasises the importance of managing thoughts and beliefs. Believers are to cast down imaginations and bring every thought into obedience to Christ, aligning their thinking with God's truth.

## Key Takeaways: The Believer's Role in the Spiritual War

THE BELIEVER'S ROLE in the spiritual war is vigilance, faith, and active engagement. Key takeaways regarding the believer's role in the spiritual war include:

1. **Responsibility of Spiritual Vigilance:** Believers are entrusted with spiritual vigilance, aware of the spiritual battle and actively guarding against the enemy's schemes.
2. **The Significance of Faith:** Faith is a fundamental component of the believer's role, enabling them to overcome the world and resist the enemy.
3. **The Believer's Weapons of Warfare:** Believers are equipped

with spiritual weapons to battle against spiritual forces, including the sword of the Spirit (the Word of God).

4. **The Power of Prayer:** Prayer is vital to the believer's role, connecting them with God and invoking His intervention in the battle.

5. **Taking Every Thought Captive:** Believers are called to manage their thoughts and beliefs, aligning them with the obedience of Christ.

The believer's role in the spiritual war is active participation, not passive observation. It calls for spiritual discernment, unwavering faith, and reliance on God's spiritual tools and weapons. As we continue to explore the implications of this cosmic battle, we will explore the biblical command to worship God alone, the pitfalls of angel worship, and the consequences of misplaced devotion.

# Chapter 6: Equipping with the Armor of God

# Exploring the Armor of God (Ephesians 6:10-18)

The "armour of God," as described in Ephesians 6:10-18, is a pivotal aspect of the believer's readiness in the spiritual war. This passage provides a comprehensive and vivid depiction of the spiritual armour that equips believers to withstand the devil's wiles and engage in the cosmic battle.

**Ephesians 6:10-18:** "Finally, be strong in the Lord, and in the strength of his might. Put on the armour of God that you can stand against the devil's wiles. For our wrestling is not against flesh and blood, but against the principalities, against the powers, against the world's rulers of the darkness of this age, and against the spiritual forces of wickedness in the heavenly places. Therefore, put on the whole armour of God so that you may be able to withstand an evil day and, having done all, stand. Stand therefore, having the utility belt of truth buckled around your waist, and having put on the breastplate of righteousness, and having fitted your feet with the preparation of the Good News of peace; above all, taking up the shield of faith, with which you will be able to quench all the fiery darts of the evil one. And take the helmet of salvation, and the sword of the Spirit, which is the word of God; with all prayer and requests, praying at all times in the Spirit, and being watchful to this end in all perseverance and requests for all the saints."

## The Call to Put On the Whole Armor of God

THE PASSAGE BEGINS with a call to action: "Finally, be strong in the Lord, and in the strength of his might." This instruction conveys the necessity of drawing strength from the Lord rather than relying on personal abilities. Believers are urged to put on the "whole armour of God" for a specific purpose: to stand against the schemes of the devil.

## Understanding the Spiritual Battle

TO FULLY APPRECIATE the significance of the "armour of God," it is crucial to understand the nature of the spiritual battle. The passage clarifies that this battle is not waged against flesh and blood but against spiritual entities and forces. These include "principalities," "powers," "world's rulers of the darkness of this age," and "spiritual forces of wickedness in the heavenly places." These entities represent the hierarchy of evil spiritual forces that oppose God's purposes.

## The Belt of Truth

THE FIRST COMPONENT of the "armour of God" is the "utility belt of truth." Just as a belt secures one's clothing, truth secures the believer's spiritual posture. This truth is not merely factual information but the truth of God's Word and the Gospel.

**John 17:17:** "Sanctify them in your truth. Your word is truth."

This verse from the Gospel of John emphasises the sanctifying power of God's truth. It sets believers apart and prepares them for the spiritual battle.

## The Breastplate of Righteousness

THE "BREASTPLATE OF righteousness" is a vital piece of armour, protecting the believer's heart and vital organs. This righteousness is not of their own making but is imputed by God through faith in Christ.

**Isaiah 61:10:** "I will greatly rejoice in Yahweh, my soul will be joyful in my God; for he has clothed me with the garments of salvation, he has covered me with the robe of righteousness, as a bridegroom decks himself with a garland, and as a bride adorns herself with her jewels."

Isaiah 61:10 beautifully portrays the believer's righteousness as a garment of salvation God provides. It signifies the covering that the breastplate of righteousness offers to the believer's spiritual core.

## Feet Shod with the Preparation of the Gospel of Peace

THE FEET SHOD WITH the preparation of the Gospel of peace indicate readiness to carry the message of peace to the world. This "armour of God" component enables believers to stand firm in their faith and share the Good News.

**Isaiah 52:7:** "How beautiful on the mountains are the feet of him who brings good news, who publishes peace, who brings good news of good, who publishes salvation, who says to Zion, 'Your God reigns!'"

This passage from Isaiah celebrates the feet of those who bring the Good News of peace. It reflects the readiness and mission of the believer to share the Gospel.

## The Shield of Faith

THE "SHIELD OF FAITH" is a prominent defensive component of the "armour of God." It serves as protection against the fiery darts of the evil one. Faith is not passive; it actively deflects and extinguishes the enemy's attacks.

**Hebrews 11:1:** "Now faith is the assurance of things hoped for, proof of things not seen."

Hebrews 11:1 defines faith as assurance and proof of things not seen. Faith is the believer's protection bedrock, providing assurance even when the enemy's attacks are unseen.

## The Helmet of Salvation

THE "HELMET OF SALVATION" guards the believer's mind and thoughts. It assures them of their eternal salvation, protecting their identity in Christ.

**1 Thessalonians 5:8:** "But let us, since we belong to the day, be sober, putting on the breastplate of faith and love, and, for a helmet, the hope of salvation."

This passage from 1 Thessalonians highlights the believer's helmet of the hope of salvation. It instils soberness and confidence, knowing that salvation is assured through Christ.

## The Sword of the Spirit: The Word of God

THE "SWORD OF THE SPIRIT" is the offensive weapon in the "armour of God." It is identified as the Word of God, highlighting the importance of Scripture in spiritual warfare.

**Hebrews 4:12:** "For the word of God is living, and active, and sharper than any two-edged sword, and piercing even to the dividing of soul and spirit, of both joints and marrow and can discern the thoughts and intentions of the heart."

Hebrews 4:12 vividly describes the power of the Word of God. It is living and active, discerning the deepest thoughts and intentions of the heart. This Word serves as the believer's offensive weapon in the spiritual battle, allowing them to cut through deception and falsehood.

## The Role of Prayer and Perseverance

THE "ARMOUR OF GOD" is not complete without prayer. Believers are encouraged to pray at all times in the Spirit, being watchful and persevering. Prayer is how they stay connected to God and to one another.

**James 5:16:** "Confess your offences to one another, and pray that you may be healed. The insistent prayer of a righteous person is powerfully effective."

James 5:16 emphasises the effectiveness of insistent prayer by righteous individuals. It brings about healing and transformation and strengthens the unity of believers.

## Key Takeaways: Exploring the Armor of God (Ephesians 6:10-18)

IN SUMMARY, THE "ARMOUR of God" described in Ephesians 6:10-18 is a comprehensive and vital aspect of the believer's readiness in the spiritual war. Key takeaways from this exploration of the armour of God include:

1. **The Call to Put On the Whole Armor of God:** Believers are urged to draw strength from the Lord and put on complete spiritual armour to stand against the devil's schemes.
2. **Understanding the Spiritual Battle:** The battle involves contending against spiritual entities and forces, not flesh and blood.
3. **The Utility Belt of Truth:** Truth is derived from God's Word and secures the believer's spiritual posture.
4. **The Breastplate of Righteousness:** Righteousness, imputed by God through faith in Christ, protects the believer's heart.
5. **Feet Shod with the Preparation of the Gospel of Peace:** Believers are ready to share the message of peace and salvation with the world.
6. **The Shield of Faith:** Faith actively deflects and extinguishes the enemy's attacks, providing assurance even in the face of the unseen.
7. **The Helmet of Salvation:** The helmet assures the believer of their eternal salvation and guards their mind and identity in Christ.
8. **The Sword of the Spirit: The Word of God:** The Word is the offensive weapon, discerning thoughts and intentions and cutting through deception and falsehood.
9. **The Role of Prayer and Perseverance:** Prayer connects believers to God and one another, bringing about healing, transformation, and unity.

The "armour of God" is a multifaceted and dynamic concept, illustrating the believer's preparedness and resilience in the spiritual war. It emphasises the importance of spiritual truth, righteousness, faith, salvation, the Word of God, and the power of prayer. As we explore the implications of the cosmic battle, we will explore the biblical command to worship God alone, the pitfalls of angel worship, and the consequences of misplaced devotion.

The "belt of truth" is the foundational piece of the "armour of God" described in Ephesians 6:10-18. In this section, we will explore the significance of the belt of truth in the believer's spiritual armour, its biblical foundations, and its practical application in the unseen struggle against spiritual forces.

**Ephesians 6:14:** "Stand, therefore, having the utility belt of truth buckled around your waist."

The "belt of truth" is introduced as an essential element of the believer's spiritual attire, symbolically fastened around the waist. This image carries deep spiritual meaning and practical relevance.

## The Symbolism of the Belt of Truth

IN ANCIENT AND MODERN times, the belt serves a practical purpose: to secure garments, especially when engaging in strenuous activity. However, in the context of the "armour of God," the belt carries profound symbolic significance:

**Securing One's Spiritual Garments:** Just as a physical belt secures clothing, the belt of truth secures the believer's spiritual garments. It holds together the other pieces of the spiritual armour, ensuring readiness for the battle.

**Truth as the Foundation:** Truth is the foundation of the believer's faith. It is the bedrock upon which their beliefs and actions are built. Without truth, the spiritual armour would lack stability and integrity.

**Discerning Deception:** A belt cinches the waist, supporting the body's core. Similarly, the belt of truth guards the core of the believer's faith and helps them discern deception and falsehood.

## Biblical Foundations of Truth

THE CONCEPT OF TRUTH has deep roots in the Bible. It is not merely a philosophical or intellectual idea but a fundamental aspect of God's character and Word.

**John 14:6:** "Jesus said to him, 'I am the way, the truth, and the life. No one comes to the Father except through me.'"

In John 14:6, Jesus unequivocally identifies Himself as "the truth." This declaration is pivotal in understanding the centrality of truth in the Christian faith. Believers are called to align with the truth embodied in Christ.

**Psalm 119:160:** "The sum of your word is truth. Every one of your righteous ordinances endures forever."

Psalm 119:160 celebrates the truth of God's Word. It emphasises that every aspect of His Word is truth, highlighting the enduring and unchanging nature of God's truth.

**John 8:31-32:** "Jesus therefore said to those Jews who had believed him, 'If you remain in my word, then you are truly my disciples. You will know the truth, and the truth will make you free.'"

Jesus connects truth with freedom in John 8:31-32. He asserts that remaining in His Word leads to knowing the truth, which results in spiritual freedom. This highlights the transformative power of truth in the believer's life.

## The Practical Application of the Belt of Truth

UNDERSTANDING THE SYMBOLISM and biblical foundations of the belt of truth, believers can apply this spiritual concept in practical ways:

**Anchoring in God's Word:** The belt of truth involves anchoring one's beliefs and actions in the truth of God's Word. Regular study and meditation on Scripture are essential for fastening this spiritual belt securely.

**Discernment of Deception:** The belt of truth equips believers to discern deception and falsehood. It empowers them to recognise and reject the lies propagated by the enemy.

**Integrity and Consistency:** Just as a physical belt holds together clothing, the belt of truth ensures that a believer's life is marked by integrity and consistency with their faith. It prevents a disconnect between what they profess and how they live.

**Protection of the Core:** The core of the body is protected by the physical belt, and in the spiritual realm, the belt of truth safeguards the core of the believer's faith. It prevents the infiltration of doubts and untruths.

**Alignment with Christ:** Recognising Jesus as "the truth" is foundational to the belt of truth. Believers are called to align their lives with the teachings and character of Christ, who is the embodiment of truth.

## Truth in the Face of Deception

THE UNSEEN STRUGGLE in the spiritual realm involves deception and spiritual warfare. The belt of truth is a vital defence against the enemy's schemes.

**2 Corinthians 11:3:** "But I am afraid that, as the serpent deceived Eve by his cunning, your minds may be corrupted from a sincere and pure devotion to Christ."

The Apostle Paul expressed concerns about deception in 2 Corinthians 11:3. Just as the serpent deceived Eve in the Garden of Eden, he feared that the minds of believers might be corrupted. The belt of truth safeguards against such corruption, ensuring a sincere and pure devotion to Christ.

**Ephesians 4:14:** "That we may no longer be children, tossed back and forth and carried about with every wind of doctrine, by the trickery of men, in craftiness, after the wiles of error."

Ephesians 4:14 warns against being "tossed back and forth" by the trickery of deceitful doctrines. The belt of truth provides stability and discernment, enabling believers to resist the "wiles of error" and remain steadfast in their faith.

## Truth in Relationships

TRUTH IS A PERSONAL virtue and a cornerstone of healthy relationships within the body of believers and those outside the faith.

**Ephesians 4:15:** "But speaking truth in love, we may grow up in all things into him who is the head, Christ."

Ephesians 4:15 encourages believers to speak the truth in love. This practice promotes growth and maturity within the body of Christ. It emphasises that truth should be communicated with compassion and respect.

**Colossians 3:9:** "Don't lie to one another, seeing that you have put off the old self with its practices."

Colossians 3:9 emphasises the importance of truthfulness in interpersonal relationships. Believers are called to honesty and transparency, rejecting falsehood and deceit.

## Key Takeaways: The Belt of Truth

THE "BELT OF TRUTH" is foundational to the believer's spiritual armour. Key takeaways regarding the belt of truth include:

1. **Symbolism of the Belt of Truth:** The belt secures the believer's spiritual garments, represents the foundation of their faith, and enables discernment.
2. **Biblical Foundations of Truth:** Truth is a core aspect of God's character and Word. Jesus Himself is identified as "the truth," and the Scriptures are celebrated as a source of enduring truth.

1.  **Practical Application:** Believers are encouraged to anchor their beliefs and actions in God's Word, discern deception, live with integrity, protect the core of their faith, and align their lives with the truth embodied in Christ.
2.  **Defence Against Deception:** The belt of truth is a vital defence against the enemy's deception schemes. It ensures that believers remain sincere and devoted to Christ, resistant to the trickery of deceitful doctrines.
3.  **Truth in Relationships:** Truth is not limited to personal integrity but also extends to relationships. Believers are called to speak the truth in love, promote growth and maturity within the body of Christ, and maintain honesty and transparency in their interactions with others.

The belt of truth is not merely a metaphorical concept but a practical and foundational aspect of the believer's spiritual life. The spiritual belt holds the rest of the "armour of God" together, providing stability, protection, and discernment. As we explore the other components of the spiritual armour, we will gain a deeper understanding of their significance in the unseen struggle against spiritual forces.

# The Breastplate of Righteousness

The "breastplate of righteousness" is a critical component of the "armour of God" described in Ephesians 6:10-18. In this section, we will explore the significance of the breastplate of righteousness in the believer's spiritual armour, its biblical foundations, and its practical application in the spiritual battle.

**Ephesians 6:14:** "Stand, therefore, having put on the breastplate of righteousness."

The breastplate of righteousness is introduced as an essential element in the believer's spiritual attire. It protects the heart and vital organs, symbolising the righteousness that guards the core of one's faith.

## The Significance of the Breastplate of Righteousness

WHETHER IN ANCIENT or modern warfare, the breastplate protects vital organs, particularly the heart. In the spiritual context, the breastplate of righteousness holds profound significance:

**Protection of the Heart:** Just as the physical breastplate safeguards the heart, the breastplate of righteousness protects the core of the believer's faith. It shields the heart from spiritual attacks and influences.

**Righteousness as a Guard:** Righteousness is not merely a characteristic but a guard against the enemy's accusations. It reassures the believer of their standing before God and defends against condemnation.

**Defence Against Accusation:** The enemy often accuses believers of unworthiness and sin in the spiritual battle. The breastplate of righteousness repels these accusations, affirming the believer's position as a child of God.

## Biblical Foundations of Righteousness

THE CONCEPT OF RIGHTEOUSNESS has deep roots in the Bible. It is an integral aspect of God's character and dealings with humanity.

**Psalm 11:7:** "For Yahweh is righteous. He loves righteousness. The upright shall see his face."

Psalm 11:7 declares the righteousness of Yahweh. He is both righteous and a lover of righteousness. This verse underlines the importance of righteousness in the believer's relationship with God.

**Isaiah 61:10:** "I will greatly rejoice in Yahweh, my soul will be joyful in my God; for he has clothed me with the garments of salvation, he has covered me with the robe of righteousness, as a bridegroom decks himself with a garland, and as a bride adorns herself with her jewels."

Isaiah 61:10 paints a vivid picture of righteousness as a robe with which God covers His people. It is a symbol of salvation and a source of great joy.

**Matthew 5:20:** "For I tell you that unless your righteousness exceeds that of the scribes and Pharisees, there is no way you will enter into the Kingdom of Heaven."

In Matthew 5:20, Jesus emphasises the importance of righteousness in entering the Kingdom of Heaven. He calls for righteousness surpassing the scribes and Pharisees' external, legalistic righteousness.

## The Practical Application of the Breastplate of Righteousness

UNDERSTANDING THE SYMBOLISM and biblical foundations of the breastplate of righteousness, believers can apply this spiritual concept in practical ways:

**Acceptance of God's Righteousness:** The breastplate of righteousness primarily involves accepting the righteousness imputed by God through faith in Christ. Believers acknowledge that their righteousness is not based on their works but on God's grace.

**Protection of the Heart and Mind:** The breastplate of righteousness guards the heart and mind, protecting them from accusations and doubts. Believers learn to repel the enemy's attempts to condemn them.

**Pursuit of Righteous Living:** While the breastplate is primarily about imputed righteousness, it encourages believers to live righteously. This means adhering to God's moral standards and striving to be conformed to His character.

**Assurance of Salvation:** The breastplate of righteousness provides assurance of salvation. Believers can rest knowing God justifies and accepts them through faith in Christ.

**Righteous Living as a Witness:** The breastplate of righteousness also has a practical aspect in the believer's witness to the world. Living a righteous life reflects God's character and draws others to Him.

## Righteousness in the Face of Accusation

THE SPIRITUAL BATTLE often involves accusations from the enemy, who seeks to condemn and discourage believers. The breastplate of righteousness plays a crucial role in countering these accusations.

**Revelation 12:10 (WEB):** "I heard a loud voice in heaven, saying, 'Now is come the salvation, the power, and the Kingdom of our God, and the authority of his Christ; for the accuser of our brothers has been thrown down, who accuses them before our God day and night.'"

Revelation 12:10 reveals the role of the accuser in the spiritual realm, who continually accuses believers before God. The breastplate of righteousness is the defence against these accusations, ensuring the believer's standing before God.

**Romans 8:33-34 (WEB):** "Who could bring a charge against God's chosen ones? It is God who justifies. Who is he who condemns?

It is Christ who died, yes rather, who was raised from the dead, who is at the right hand of God, who also makes intercession for us."

Romans 8:33-34 provides assurance in the face of accusation. No charge can be brought against God's chosen ones because God justifies them. Christ intercedes for believers, reinforcing their righteousness and protecting them from condemnation.

## Righteousness in Relationships

THE BREASTPLATE OF righteousness extends its impact to the believer's interactions with others, promoting healthy relationships and a godly witness.

**Proverbs 11:20 (WEB):** "Those who are perverse in heart are an abomination to Yahweh, but those whose ways are blameless are his delight."

Proverbs 11:20 highlights the delight of the Lord in those whose ways are blameless. Righteous living protects the believer's heart and brings delight to God.

**1 Timothy 6:11 (WEB):** "But you, man of God, flee these things, and follow after righteousness, godliness, faith, love, patience, and gentleness."

In 1 Timothy 6:11, believers are encouraged to pursue righteousness as one of the qualities that define a person of God. Righteousness is an essential component of godly character.

## Key Takeaways: The Breastplate of Righteousness

IN SUMMARY, THE "BREASTPLATE of righteousness" is a fundamental component of the believer's spiritual armour. Key takeaways regarding the breastplate of righteousness include:

1. **Significance of the Breastplate of Righteousness:** The breastplate protects the heart and vital organs, symbolising the righteousness that guards the core of the believer's faith

and serves as a defence against accusation and condemnation.

2. **Biblical Foundations of Righteousness:** Righteousness is deeply rooted in the character of God and His Word. It is imputed through faith in Christ and a call to live righteously.

3. **Practical Application:** Believers apply the breastplate of righteousness by accepting God's imputed righteousness, protecting their hearts and minds, living righteously, finding assurance in their salvation, and being a witness through righteous living.

4. **Righteousness in the Face of Accusation:** The breastplate of righteousness serves as a defence against the enemy's accusations. It reinforces the believer's standing before God and their justification through Christ.

5. **Righteousness in Relationships:** Righteous living also extends to relationships, fostering healthy interactions and witnessing God's delight in righteous living.

The breastplate of righteousness is a spiritual defence that safeguards the believer's heart and stands as a symbol of God's imputed righteousness and the call to live righteously. As we explore the other components of the spiritual armour, we will gain a deeper understanding of their significance in the unseen struggle against spiritual forces.

# The Shoes of the Gospel of Peace

The "shoes of the gospel of peace" constitute a pivotal element in the "armour of God," as outlined in Ephesians 6:10-18. In this section, we will explore the significance of the shoes of the gospel of peace in the believer's spiritual armour, its biblical foundations, and its practical application in the spiritual battle.

**Ephesians 6:15:** "And having fitted your feet with the preparation of the gospel of peace."

The shoes of the gospel of peace are introduced as an essential component of the believer's spiritual attire. They symbolise readiness, mobility, and the foundation of peace upon which the believer stands in the spiritual battle.

## The Symbolism of the Shoes of the Gospel of Peace

IN BOTH ANCIENT AND modern contexts, footwear serves the purpose of protection and mobility. In the spiritual realm, the shoes of the gospel of peace hold profound symbolic significance:

**Readiness for Movement:** Just as physical shoes enable movement, the shoes of the gospel of peace signify readiness for action in the spiritual battle. Believers are prepared to carry the message of peace wherever they go.

**Foundation of Peace:** The shoes represent the foundation of peace upon which the believer stands. In a turbulent and tumultuous world, the gospel of peace provides a firm footing, assuring believers of their position in Christ.

**Proclamation of Peace:** Shoes are worn when one goes out into the world, and the shoes of the gospel of peace symbolise the believer's role in proclaiming the message of peace to a world in need.

## Biblical Foundations of the Gospel of Peace

THE CONCEPT OF PEACE and the gospel's role in bringing peace are deeply rooted in the Bible. It is a theme throughout Scripture, reflecting God's character and redemptive plan.

**Isaiah 52:7:** "How beautiful on the mountains are the feet of him who brings good news, who publishes peace, who brings good news of good, who publishes salvation, who says to Zion, 'Your God reigns!'"

Isaiah 52:7 portrays the beauty of those who publish good news and peace. This verse speaks to the role of messengers who herald the gospel of peace and declare God's reign.

**Romans 5:1:** "Being therefore justified by faith, we have peace with God through our Lord Jesus Christ."

Romans 5:1 highlights the peace with God that believers experience through justification by faith. The gospel brings reconciliation, establishing peace between God and humanity.

**Ephesians 2:14 (WEB):** "For he is our peace, who made both one, and broke down the middle wall of separation."

Ephesians 2:14 refers to Christ as our peace, the One who has broken down the barriers that separated us from God and one another. The gospel reconciles and unites, bringing peace.

## The Practical Application of the Shoes of the Gospel of Peace

UNDERSTANDING THE SYMBOLISM and biblical foundations of the shoes of the gospel of peace, believers can apply this spiritual concept in practical ways:

**Readiness for Evangelism:** The shoes of the gospel of peace symbolise readiness for evangelism. Believers prepare to share the message of peace and salvation with others, recognising the task's urgency.

**Firm Foundation in Peace:** Just as shoes provide a stable footing, the shoes of the gospel of peace remind believers to stand firmly on the foundation of peace found in Christ. In times of turbulence and uncertainty, this foundation offers assurance and stability.

**Proclamation of Peace:** Believers are called to be messengers of peace, sharing the good news of salvation and reconciliation. This proclamation is not limited to words but is demonstrated through actions and lifestyle.

**Trusting God's Sovereignty:** The shoes of the gospel of peace encourage trust in God's sovereignty and the fact that He reigns. This trust provides peace in life's challenges and uncertainties.

## Spreading Peace in a Troubled World

THE WORLD IS OFTEN marked by conflict, discord, and a lack of peace. The shoes of the gospel of peace empower believers to bring the message of peace to a troubled world.

**Matthew 5:9 (WEB):** "Blessed are the peacemakers, for they shall be called children of God."

In Matthew 5:9, Jesus pronounces a blessing on peacemakers, identifying them as children of God. Believers who actively spread the message of peace become agents of reconciliation, reflecting God's character.

**2 Corinthians 5:18:** "But all things are of God, who reconciled us to himself through Jesus Christ, and gave us the ministry of reconciliation."

2 Corinthians 5:18 emphasises that believers have been given the ministry of reconciliation. This ministry involves sharing the message of peace and reconciliation found in Christ.

**Romans 10:15:** "And how will they preach unless they are sent? As it is written: 'How beautiful are the feet of those who preach the gospel of peace, who bring glad tidings of good things!'"

Romans 10:15 echoes the sentiment of Isaiah 52:7, celebrating the beauty of those who preach the gospel of peace. It emphasises the vital role of messengers who bring glad tidings of good things.

## Key Takeaways: The Shoes of the Gospel of Peace

IN SUMMARY, THE "SHOES of the gospel of peace" are a significant element of the believer's spiritual armour. Key takeaways regarding the shoes of the gospel of peace include:

1. **Symbolism of the Shoes of the Gospel of Peace:** The shoes symbolise readiness for action, a firm foundation of peace, and the believer's role in proclaiming the message of peace to the world.
2. **Biblical Foundations of the Gospel of Peace:** Peace is deeply rooted in the Bible, reflecting God's character and redemptive plan. The gospel brings reconciliation and unites people in peace.
3. **Practical Application:** Believers are encouraged to be ready for evangelism, find a firm foundation in the peace of Christ, actively proclaim the message of peace, and trust in God's sovereignty.
4. **Spreading Peace in a Troubled World:** The shoes of the gospel of peace empower believers to be peacemakers, engage in the ministry of reconciliation, and bring the good news of peace to a world in need.

The shoes of the gospel of peace remind believers that they are messengers of peace in a troubled world, called to share the message of reconciliation and to stand firmly on the foundation of peace found in Christ. As we explore the other components of the spiritual armour, we will gain a deeper understanding of their significance in the unseen struggle against spiritual forces.

The "shield of faith" plays a crucial role in the "armour of God" described in Ephesians 6:10-18. In this section, we will explore the significance of the shield of faith in the believer's spiritual armour, its biblical foundations, and its practical application in the spiritual battle.

**Ephesians 6:16:** "Above all, taking up the shield of faith, with which you will be able to quench all the fiery darts of the evil one."

The shield of faith is an indispensable element in the believer's spiritual attire. It symbolises protection, defence, and the unwavering trust that shields against the enemy's attacks.

## The Symbolism of the Shield of Faith

SHIELDS HAVE BEEN USED throughout history as protective barriers against enemy attacks. In the spiritual context, the shield of faith holds deep symbolic meaning:

**Protection from Attacks:** Just as physical shields protect soldiers from enemy projectiles, the shield of faith guards the believer from the assaults of the evil one. It provides a barrier against spiritual attacks and temptations.

**Faith as a Defence:** Faith is not merely a belief but a powerful defence mechanism. It acts as a shield, intercepting and extinguishing the "fiery darts" launched by the enemy.

**Unwavering Trust:** The shield of faith represents unwavering trust in God. It is a declaration of confidence in His promises, character, and protection.

## Biblical Foundations of Faith as a Shield

THE CONCEPT OF FAITH as a shield has its roots in the Bible, where faith is portrayed as a powerful force that protects and sustains believers.

**Psalm 91:4 (WEB):** "He will cover you with his feathers. Under his wings, you will take refuge. His faithfulness is your shield and rampart."

In Psalm 91:4, faithfulness is portrayed as a shield and rampart. God's faithfulness is the believer's protection, offering refuge under His wings.

**Hebrews 11:1 (WEB):** "Now faith is the assurance of things hoped for, proof of things not seen."

Hebrews 11:1 defines faith as the assurance of things hoped for and the proof of things not seen. This verse emphasises the core nature of faith as trust in the unseen, which serves as a powerful shield against doubt and uncertainty.

**1 Peter 1:5 (WEB):** "Who by the power of God are guarded through faith for a salvation ready to be revealed in the last time."

1 Peter 1:5 speaks of believers being guarded through faith. Faith acts as a guard, protecting them in anticipation of the salvation to be revealed.

## The Practical Application of the Shield of Faith

UNDERSTANDING THE SYMBOLISM and biblical foundations of the shield of faith, believers can apply this spiritual concept in practical ways:

**Confidence in God's Promises:** The shield of faith involves unwavering confidence in God's promises. Believers must actively trust in His Word and rely on His faithfulness.

**Protection from Attacks:** Faith serves as a protective shield against the enemy's attacks, including doubt, fear, and temptation.

Believers use their faith to deflect these assaults and stand firm in their trust in God.

**Declaration of Trust:** The shield of faith is a declaration of trust. It requires believers to boldly proclaim their unwavering confidence in God's character and sovereignty.

**Acting on Faith:** Faith is not passive but active. Believers must act on their faith by obeying God's commands, stepping out in courage, and living according to their trust in Him.

## Faith as a Defense Against Doubt and Fear

THE SHIELD OF FAITH is particularly effective in countering doubt and fear, two common weapons the enemy uses in the spiritual battle.

**James 1:6:** "But let him ask in faith, without any doubting, for he who doubts is like a wave of the sea, driven by the wind and tossed."

James 1:6 highlights the importance of asking in faith without doubting. Doubt makes a person unstable and easily swayed. The shield of faith provides stability and confidence in prayer and decision-making.

**2 Timothy 1:7:** "For God didn't give us a spirit of fear but of power, love, and self-control."

In 2 Timothy 1:7, it's clear that fear does not come from God. The shield of faith counters fear by reinforcing the believer's understanding of God's power, love, and self-control.

## Trusting in God's Protection

THE SHIELD OF FAITH encourages believers to trust in God's protection, even in the face of adversity and danger.

**Psalm 28:7:** "Yahweh is my strength and shield. My heart has trusted in him, and I am helped. Therefore, my heart greatly rejoices. With my song, I will thank him."

Psalm 28:7 expresses trust in Yahweh as both strength and shield. Trusting in God leads to help and rejoicing, even in challenging circumstances.

**Psalm 33:20 (WEB):** "Our soul has waited for Yahweh. He is our help and our shield."

Psalm 33:20 affirms that Yahweh is the source of help and protection for those who wait on Him. The shield of faith encourages patience and reliance on God's timing and intervention.

## Key Takeaways: The Shield of Faith

IN SUMMARY, THE "SHIELD of faith" is a fundamental component of the believer's spiritual armour. Key takeaways regarding the shield of faith include:

1. **Symbolism of the Shield of Faith:** The shield protects believers from spiritual attacks, represents unwavering trust, and acts as a defence against the enemy's assaults.

2. **Biblical Foundations of Faith as a Shield:** Faith is deeply rooted in the Bible as the assurance of the unseen, protection through God's faithfulness, and a powerful force that guards and sustains believers.

3. **Practical Application:** The shield of faith involves confidence in God's promises, protection from attacks, the declaration of trust, and active obedience to God's commands.

4. **Faith as a Defense Against Doubt and Fear:** Faith counters doubt and fear, providing stability, confidence in prayer and decision-making, and trust in God's power and love.

5. **Trusting in God's Protection:** The shield of faith encourages believers to trust in God's protection, seek His help, rejoice in His strength, and wait on Him.

The shield of faith is a powerful spiritual defence that protects believers from doubt, fear, and the enemy's attacks. It symbolises unwavering trust in God and His promises. As we continue to explore the other components of the spiritual armour, we will gain a deeper understanding of

## Using the Shield of Faith in Spiritual Warfare

AS BELIEVERS NAVIGATE the spiritual battle, it's essential to actively and effectively use the shield of faith in practical ways:

**1. Regularly Feed Your Faith:** Just as physical strength requires nourishment, your faith needs regular feeding. This involves reading and meditating on God's Word, prayer, and cultivating a deep relationship with Him. A well-nourished faith is a strong shield.

**2. Declare God's Promises:** The shield of faith is also a declaration of trust in God's promises. In challenges and spiritual attacks, proclaim and stand on God's promises. This active declaration strengthens your faith and serves as a powerful defence.

**3. Resist Doubt and Fear:** Doubt and fear are common enemy tactics. When faced with uncertainty or anxiety, use your shield of faith to resist these attacks. Remind yourself of God's faithfulness and trustworthiness.

**4. Act Courageously:** Faith is not passive. It propels you to act courageously, even in the face of adversity. When God calls you to step out in faith, do so with confidence, knowing that your shield of faith will protect you.

**5. Encourage Others:** Just as a formation of soldiers can create a formidable shield wall, a community of believers can provide mutual support and encouragement. Encourage fellow believers in their faith and stand strong against the enemy's attacks.

## Trusting in God's Unseen Protection

FAITH IS OFTEN ABOUT trusting in the unseen and believing in God's invisible hand. In the spiritual battle, this trust is the core of the shield of faith.

**2 Corinthians 4:18:** "While we don't look at the things which are seen, but at the things which are not seen. For the things seen are temporal, but those not seen are eternal."

The shield of faith directs our focus to the eternal and unseen realities. It reminds us that our trust in God's protection is not based on visible circumstances but on His unchanging character and promises.

**Hebrews 11:6:** "Without faith, it is impossible to be well pleasing to him, for he who comes to God must believe that he exists and that he is a rewarder of those who seek him."

Hebrews 11:6 emphasises the foundational nature of faith in our relationship with God. It requires believing in His existence and trusting that He rewards those who seek Him. This trust forms the core of our shield of faith.

• • • •

THE SHIELD OF FAITH is not just a symbolic piece of the believer's spiritual armour; it's a powerful and practical tool in the unseen struggle against spiritual forces. You are fortified against doubt, fear, and the enemy's fiery darts as you wield this shield. Trust in God's promises and faithfulness is a formidable defence, allowing you to stand strong in adversity.

In the spiritual battle, the shield of faith reminds us that we are not alone. We have a reliable and unchanging source of protection. As we explore the other components of spiritual armour, we will gain a deeper understanding of their significance and how they equip believers to face the challenges of the unseen struggle.

The next component of the spiritual armour we will explore is "The Helmet of Salvation," which guards the believer's mind and thoughts, providing protection and assurance in the spiritual battle.

# The Helmet of Salvation

In the spiritual battle against the forces of darkness, the "helmet of salvation" is vital to the "armour of God." This section will explore the significance of the helmet of salvation in the believer's spiritual armour, its biblical foundations, and its practical application in the ongoing struggle.

**Ephesians 6:17:** "And take the helmet of salvation."

The helmet of salvation is crucial to the believer's spiritual attire. It symbolises protection, assurance, and guarding the mind against enemy attacks.

## The Symbolism of the Helmet of Salvation

HELMETS HAVE BEEN A vital piece of protective gear for soldiers throughout history, guarding the head against potentially fatal blows. In the spiritual context, the helmet of salvation carries profound symbolism:

**Protection of the Mind:** Just as physical helmets shield the head, the seat of intellect and thought, the helmet of salvation protects the believer's mind from spiritual attacks and doubts.

**Assurance of Salvation:** The helmet symbolises the assurance of salvation. Believers are reminded of their secure position in Christ, preventing doubts about their salvation.

**Guarding Against Deception:** The helmet defends the believer's thought processes, guarding against deception and false teachings that may lead them astray.

## Biblical Foundations of the Helmet of Salvation

THE CONCEPT OF SALVATION is foundational to the Christian faith and profoundly impacts the believer's identity and mindset.

**1 Thessalonians 5:8:** "But let us, since we belong to the day, be sober, putting on the breastplate of faith and love, and for a helmet, the hope of salvation."

In 1 Thessalonians 5:8, the helmet is described as the "hope of salvation." This hope is a source of protection, keeping the believer's mind focused on the promise of eternal salvation.

**Romans 8:38-39:** "For I am persuaded that neither death, nor life, nor angels, nor principalities, nor things present, nor things to come, nor powers, nor height, nor depth, nor any other created thing will be able to separate us from the love of God, which is in Christ Jesus our Lord."

Romans 8:38-39 highlights the unbreakable bond between believers and God through Christ. The assurance of this eternal love provides a solid foundation for the believer's confidence in their salvation.

**2 Timothy 1:12:** "For this cause I suffer also these things. Yet I am not ashamed, for I know him whom I have believed, and I am persuaded that he can guard that which I have committed to him against that day."

In 2 Timothy 1:12, the Apostle Paul expresses his unwavering confidence in the Lord's ability to guard what he has committed, referring to his salvation. This verse emphasises the certainty and security of salvation.

## The Practical Application of the Helmet of Salvation

UNDERSTANDING THE SYMBOLISM and biblical foundations of the helmet of salvation, believers can apply this spiritual concept in practical ways:

**1. Assurance of Salvation:** Regularly reflect on your salvation experience and the faithfulness of God. Understand that your salvation is not based on feelings but on the unchanging promise of God.

**2. Guard Your Thoughts:** Actively guard your thoughts against doubts, fears, and deceptions. When negative or misleading thoughts arise, counter them with the truth of God's Word and the assurance of salvation.

**3. Firm Identity in Christ:** Recognise your identity is securely rooted in Christ. Your salvation depends not on your performance but on Christ's finished work on the cross.

**4. Resist Deception:** Be discerning and cautious about false teachings or beliefs that may undermine your confidence in salvation. A well-fitted helmet of salvation helps resist such attacks.

## Guarding the Mind Against Doubt and Deception

IN THE SPIRITUAL BATTLE, the helmet of salvation is instrumental in guarding the believer's mind against doubt and deception.

**2 Corinthians 10:5:** "Casting down imaginations and every high thing that is exalted against the knowledge of God, and bringing every thought into captivity to the obedience of Christ."

This verse encourages believers to take control of their thoughts and bring them into obedience to Christ. The helmet of salvation equips you to cast down thoughts opposing God's knowledge.

**Philippians 4:7:** "And the peace of God, which surpasses all understanding, will guard your hearts and thoughts in Christ Jesus."

Philippians 4:7 illustrates the role of God's peace in guarding the believer's thoughts. This peace is rooted in salvation and assures believers of their position in Christ.

## A Firm Foundation for Confidence and Assurance

THE HELMET OF SALVATION provides a firm foundation for believers to have confidence and assurance in their faith, even in spiritual battles and doubts.

**John 10:28:** "I give eternal life to them, and they will never perish. No one will snatch them out of my hand."

In John 10:28, Jesus affirms the eternal security of those in His care. The helmet of salvation reinforces the belief that no one can snatch believers from His hand.

**1 John 5:13:** "These things I have written to you who believe in the name of the Son of God, that you may know that you have eternal life and that you may continue to believe in the name of the Son of God."

The Apostle John emphasises the assurance of eternal life. The helmet of salvation lets believers know with confidence that they have eternal life in Christ.

## Key Takeaways: The Helmet of Salvation

THE "HELMET OF SALVATION" is crucial to the believer's spiritual armour. Key takeaways regarding the Helmet of Salvation include:

1. **Symbolism of the Helmet of Salvation:** The helmet protects the believer's mind, provides assurance of salvation, and guards against deception and doubt.
2. **Biblical Foundations of the Helmet of Salvation:** Salvation is central to the Christian faith, and the believer's security is rooted in God's unchanging promise.
3. **Practical Application:** Believers should regularly reflect on their salvation, guard their thoughts, understand their identity in Christ, and resist deception.
4. **Guarding the Mind Against Doubt and Deception:** The helmet of salvation equips believers to cast down thoughts opposing the knowledge of God and brings every thought into obedience to Christ.
5. **A Firm Foundation for Confidence and Assurance:** The helmet of salvation provides a firm foundation for believers

to have confidence and assurance in their faith, rooted in the unchanging promise of God.

The helmet of salvation guards the believer's mind against doubt and deception, providing a secure foundation for confidence and assurance in their faith. As we explore the other components of the spiritual armour, we will gain a deeper understanding of their significance in the ongoing struggle against spiritual forces.

In the spiritual battle against the forces of darkness, the "sword of the Spirit" is a formidable and indispensable weapon in the "armour of God." In this section, we will explore the significance of the sword of the Spirit in the believer's spiritual armour, its biblical foundations, and its practical application in the ongoing struggle.

**Ephesians 6:17:** "And take the helmet of salvation, and the sword of the Spirit, which is the word of God."

The sword of the Spirit is introduced as a vital element in the believer's spiritual attire. It symbolises God's Word's power, precision, and effectiveness in the spiritual battle.

## The Symbolism of the Sword of the Spirit

A SWORD IS A WEAPON of offence and defence. In the spiritual context, the sword of the Spirit carries deep symbolic meaning:

**The Word of God:** The sword symbolises the Word of God, which is sharp, living, and active (Hebrews 4:12). It is a powerful weapon penetrating the deepest parts of the human heart and mind.

**Offensive and Defensive:** A sword can be used both offensively and defensively. Similarly, the Word of God confronts and exposes the enemy's tactics while providing comfort, encouragement, and guidance to the believer.

**Precision and Effectiveness:** Swords require skill and precision to wield effectively. The believer must be well-versed in God's Word, using it with accuracy and discernment in the spiritual battle.

## Biblical Foundations of the Sword of the Spirit

THE CONCEPT OF THE Word of God as a weapon and source of spiritual power is deeply rooted in the Bible.

**Hebrews 4:12:** "For the word of God is living, and active, and sharper than any two-edged sword, and piercing even to the dividing of soul and spirit, of both joints and marrow and can discern the thoughts and intentions of the heart."

Hebrews 4:12 vividly describes the Word of God as living, active, and sharper than any two-edged sword. It has the power to discern thoughts and intentions, revealing the depth of its impact.

**2 Timothy 3:16-17:** "Every Scripture is God-breathed and profitable for teaching, for reproof, for correction, and for instruction in righteousness, that the man of God may be complete, thoroughly equipped for every good work."

In 2 Timothy 3:16-17, the Scriptures are presented as God-breathed and profoundly useful for various aspects of the believer's life. They equip believers for every good work and empower them to fight spiritual battles.

**Matthew 4:4:** "But he answered, 'It is written, "Man shall not live by bread alone, but by every word that proceeds out of the mouth of God."'"

During His temptation in the wilderness, Jesus emphasised the significance of the Word of God. He relied on Scripture to respond to the enemy's attacks, demonstrating the power of God's Word as a weapon in spiritual warfare.

## The Practical Application of the Sword of the Spirit

UNDERSTANDING THE SYMBOLISM and biblical foundations of the sword of the Spirit, believers can apply this spiritual concept in practical ways:

**1. Study God's Word:** To wield the sword effectively, believers must regularly and diligently study God's Word. This includes reading, meditating, and memorising Scripture.

**2. Use the Word in Prayer:** Incorporate God's Word into your prayers. Pray Scripture over situations, seeking God's wisdom, guidance, and intervention.

**3. Engage in Spiritual Battle:** The sword of the Spirit is meant for battle. When faced with spiritual attacks, temptations, or doubts, use Scripture to confront the enemy's lies and deceptions.

**4. Comfort and Encourage:** The Word of God is not just for battle; it also provides comfort and encouragement. Share relevant passages with fellow believers who are facing trials and difficulties.

## The Power of the Sword of the Spirit

THE SWORD OF THE SPIRIT holds immense power, enabling believers to overcome spiritual challenges, confront the enemy's tactics, and experience transformation.

**Psalm 119:105:** "Your word is a lamp to my feet and a light for my path."

Psalm 119:105 illustrates how the Word of God is a lamp to guide one's steps and a light for one's path. In darkness and confusion, the Word illuminates the way.

**Isaiah 55:11:** "So will my word be that goes out of my mouth: it will not return to me void, but it will accomplish that which I please, and it will prosper in the thing I sent it to do."

Isaiah 55:11 emphasises the effectiveness of God's Word. It is not empty or void; it accomplishes His purpose and prospers in the tasks for which it is sent. This highlights the Word's inherent power and efficacy.

**John 8:31-32:** "Jesus therefore said to those Jews who had believed in him, 'If you remain in my word, then you are truly my disciples. You will know the truth, and the truth will make you free.'"

In John 8:31-32, Jesus speaks of the liberating power of the truth in His Word. Remaining in His Word leads to genuine discipleship, knowledge of the truth, and ultimate freedom.

## The Sword of the Spirit in the Unseen Struggle

THE SWORD OF THE SPIRIT is a dynamic and transformative tool in the hands of believers in the unseen struggle. It enables them to:

**1. Confront Lies and Deceptions:** The enemy often employs lies and deceptions in the spiritual battle. The Word of God exposes falsehood and provides clarity.

**2. Resist Temptations:** When tempted, believers can use Scripture to resist and overcome the allure of sin. It is a powerful weapon to stay on the path of righteousness.

**3. Experience Transformation:** The Word of God can transform hearts and minds. It convicts, corrects, and guides believers in their journey of faith.

**4. Lead Others to Truth:** Sharing the Word of God with others is a way to lead them to the truth and point them to Christ, the ultimate source of salvation.

## Key Takeaways: The Sword of the Spirit

THE "SWORD OF THE SPIRIT" is a dynamic and potent component of the believer's spiritual armour. Key takeaways regarding the sword of the Spirit include:

1. **Symbolism of the Sword of the Spirit:** The sword represents the Word of God. This powerful and versatile weapon is both offensive and defensive.

2. **Biblical Foundations of the Sword of the Spirit:** The Word of God is described as living, sharp, and able to discern thoughts and intentions. It is profitable for teaching, reproof, correction, and instruction in righteousness.

3. **Practical Application:** Believers should study, use, and engage in spiritual battle with the Word of God. It is a source of comfort, encouragement, and transformation.

4. **The Power of the Sword of the Spirit:** God's Word is a

guiding light, accomplishes His purpose, and sets believers free. It has the power to transform lives and lead people to the truth.

The sword of the Spirit, the Word of God, equips believers to confront lies, resist temptations, experience transformation, and lead others to truth in the ongoing spiritual battle. As we explore the remaining components of the spiritual armour, we will gain a deeper understanding of their significance in the unseen struggle against spiritual forces.

# Praying with the help of the Holy Spirit

Prayer is a fundamental aspect of the Christian faith and is crucial to the believer's spiritual armour. Praying with the Spirit's help is a concept deeply rooted in Scripture, and it is vital in the ongoing spiritual battle against the forces of darkness. This section will explore the significance of praying in the Spirit, its biblical foundations, and how it empowers believers in the unseen struggle. However, right at the outset, the emphasis must be placed on the correct understanding of praying in the Spirit. "Praying in the Spirit," as emphasised in Ephesians 6:18, refers to praying with the assistance and guidance of the Holy Spirit. This form of prayer is deeply rooted in Christian tradition. It is believed to enable believers to communicate directly with God in a manner that aligns with His will. However, it's crucial to differentiate this sacred practice from certain manifestations sometimes associated with it in some churches, where individuals may exhibit uncontrollable laughter or behave disorderly. Such conduct can lead to misunderstandings about the true nature of praying in the Spirit. Instead, the essence of this type of prayer lies in seeking divine guidance, wisdom, and connection with God, with reverence and respect for His holiness, as exemplified in passages like Romans 8:26-27, which emphasises the Spirit's role in aiding believers in their prayers.

**Ephesians 6:18:** "Praying at all times in the Spirit, with all prayer and supplication. To that end, be alert with all perseverance and supplication for all the saints."

Praying in the Spirit is introduced in Ephesians 6:18 as an essential component of the believer's spiritual warfare. It is an ongoing practice that connects believers with God and empowers them for the battle.

## The Significance of Praying in the Spirit

PRAYING IN THE SPIRIT holds profound significance in the spiritual battle:

**Communion with God:** It is a means of communing with God and deepening the believer's relationship with Him. Prayer is the believer's direct line of communication with their Heavenly Father.

**Empowerment:** Praying in the Spirit empowers the believer with spiritual strength, wisdom, and discernment to face the challenges and deceptions of the enemy.

**Spiritual Sensitivity:** It sharpens the believer's spiritual sensitivity, enabling them to discern the Holy Spirit's movements and the enemy's tactics.

**Intercession:** Praying in the Spirit includes intercession for oneself and for others, lifting up fellow believers in prayer and seeking God's protection, guidance, and blessing.

## Biblical Foundations of Praying in the Spirit

THE PRACTICE OF PRAYING in the Spirit is deeply rooted in the Bible, with multiple references that illuminate its significance:

**Romans 8:26-27:** "In the same way, the Spirit also helps our weaknesses, for we don't know how to pray as we ought. But the Spirit makes intercession for us with groanings that can't be uttered. He who searches the hearts knows what is on the Spirit's mind because he makes intercession for the saints according to God."

Romans 8:26-27 reveals that the Holy Spirit assists believers in prayer, especially in moments of weakness when they may not know how to pray. The Spirit intercedes for the saints by God's will.

**Jude 1:20:** "But you, beloved, keep building yourselves on your most holy faith, praying in the Holy Spirit."

Jude encourages believers to build faith by praying in the Holy Spirit. This form of prayer is essential for spiritual growth and strength.

**1 Corinthians 14:14-15:** "For if I pray in another language, my spirit prays, but my understanding is unfruitful. What is it then? I will pray with the spirit, and I will pray with the understanding also. I will sing with the spirit, and I will sing with the understanding also."

The Apostle Paul discusses praying in tongues or another language in 1 Corinthians 14. He highlights that this form of prayer engages the spirit and can be coupled with understanding for edification and praise.

**Ephesians 6:18:** "Praying at all times in the Spirit, with all prayer and supplication."

In Ephesians 6:18, the command to pray at all times in the Spirit is directly connected to spiritual armour. It emphasises the importance of this practice in the ongoing spiritual battle.

## The Practical Application of Praying in the Spirit

PRAYING IN THE SPIRIT is a dynamic and transformative practice that can be applied in various ways:

**1. Regular Communion:** Develop a habit of regular communion with God through prayer. This includes asking for needs and seeking His presence and guidance.

**2. Intercession:** Pray for fellow believers, the Church, and the world's needs. Intercession is a powerful way to support others in the spiritual battle.

**3. Seeking Discernment:** When faced with challenging decisions or spiritual battles, seek discernment from the Holy Spirit through prayer. Ask for wisdom and guidance.

## The Empowerment of Praying with the Spirit's help

PRAYING IN THE SPIRIT empowers believers in various ways:

**1. Strength in Weakness:** When believers don't know how to pray, the Holy Spirit intercedes, providing strength in moments of weakness.

**2. Spiritual Growth:** Regular prayer in the Spirit leads to spiritual growth, deepening the believer's faith and relationship with God.

**3. Discernment:** Praying in the Spirit sharpens spiritual discernment, enabling believers to recognise the Holy Spirit's movements and the enemy's strategies.

**4. Unity and Intercession:** Intercession for fellow believers fosters unity within the Church and reinforces community bonds as believers stand together in the unseen struggle.

## Key Takeaways: Praying with the Spirit's help

"PRAYING IN THE SPIRIT" is a foundational and dynamic aspect of the believer's spiritual life and warfare. Key takeaways regarding praying in the Spirit include:

1. **Significance of Praying in the Spirit:** It facilitates communion with God, empowers the believer, sharpens spiritual sensitivity, and enables intercession.
2. **Biblical Foundations:** The Bible highlights the role of the Holy Spirit in intercession and encourages praying in the Holy Spirit.
3. **Practical Application:** Believers should engage in regular communion with God, intercede for others, seek discernment, and, if gifted, practice praying in tongues.
4. **Empowerment:** Praying in the Spirit strengthens weakness, fosters spiritual growth, enhances discernment, and encourages unity through intercession.

Praying in the Spirit is a powerful tool for believers navigating the unseen struggle against spiritual forces. As we explore the remaining components of the spiritual armour, we will gain a deeper understanding of their significance and practical application in the ongoing battle.

# Chapter 7: Practical Applications

# How to Recognise Angelic and Demonic Influences

In the unseen struggle between angels and demons, believers must discern the influences at play. This section explores how to recognise angelic and demonic influences in our lives and the world, drawing insights from Scripture and practical application.

**1 Corinthians 14:33:** "For God is not a God of confusion but of peace."

God is a God of order and peace. Understanding the influences of angels and demons can help bring clarity to spiritual battles.

## Discerning Angelic Influences

ANGELIC INFLUENCES are often characterised by the following:

**1. Peace and Comfort:** Angels often bring peace and comfort. In moments of distress, their presence can be calming.

**2. Guidance and Protection:** Angels may guide and protect believers. They intervene to ensure God's will is fulfilled in one's life.

**3. Messages in Line with Scripture:** Angelic messages align with the teachings of Scripture. They will never contradict God's Word.

**4. Encouragement and Edification:** Angels bring encouragement and edification. Their presence or messages uplift and strengthen the believer.

**5. Aligning with God's Will:** Angelic influences are in harmony with God's divine plan for the believer's life.

**Matthew 18:10:** "See that you don't despise one of these little ones, for I tell you that in heaven, their angels always see the face of my Father who is in heaven."

This verse reveals that believers, especially children, have guardian angels who continuously stand before God. Angelic protection and guidance are a constant presence in their lives.

# Discerning Demonic Influences

DEMONIC INFLUENCES can manifest in various ways:

**1. Confusion and Fear:** Demons often bring confusion, fear, and chaos. Their presence disrupts peace and order.

**2. Temptation and Deception:** Demonic influences may tempt believers to sin or lead them into deception. They twist God's truth to mislead.

**3. Discord and Division:** Demons thrive on discord and division within relationships and communities. They sow seeds of bitterness and conflict.

**4. Oppression and Torment:** Demonic influences may lead to oppression and torment. This can manifest as unexplained physical or mental anguish.

**5. Contradiction to God's Word:** Demonic influences lead people away from God's Word and principles. They promote falsehood and rebellion.

**Ephesians 6:12:** "For our wrestling is not against flesh and blood, but against the principalities, against the powers, against the world's rulers of the darkness of this age, and against the spiritual forces of wickedness in the heavenly places."

Ephesians 6:12 emphasises the spiritual nature of the battle. Demonic influences are part of the "spiritual forces of wickedness" that believers confront.

# The Importance of Biblical Discernment

DISCERNING THESE INFLUENCES requires a strong foundation in the Bible. The Word of God is a reliable source for discerning what aligns with His will.

**Hebrews 5:14:** "But solid food is for those who are full grown, who because of use have their senses exercised to discern good and evil."

Mature believers who have "their senses exercised" can discern between good and evil. This discernment comes from continually immersing themselves in God's Word.

**1 John 4:1:** "Beloved, don't believe every spirit, but test the spirits, whether they are of God because many false prophets have gone out into the world."

Testing the spirits means evaluating influences and messages against the truth of Scripture. This is crucial in discerning whether they are from God or not.

## Practical Steps for Discernment

TO DISCERN ANGELIC and demonic influences effectively, believers can take practical steps:

**1. Prayer:** Seek guidance through prayer. Ask God for wisdom and discernment to recognise the sources of influence.

**2. Test Against Scripture:** Always compare messages, experiences, or influences with the teachings of the Bible. If it contradicts God's Word, it's not from Him.

**3. Seek Accountability:** Discuss experiences or influences with trusted fellow believers or spiritual mentors. They can offer valuable perspectives and guidance.

**4. Focus on the Fruit:** Assess the fruit or results of influences. Does it lead to love, joy, peace, patience, kindness, goodness, faithfulness, gentleness, and self-control (Galatians 5:22-23)?

**5. Pray for Protection:** Regularly pray for God's protection from negative influences and the discernment to recognise them.

**1 Thessalonians 5:21 (WEB):** "Test all things, and hold firmly that which is good."

This verse encourages believers to test everything and hold onto what is good. Discernment is an active process of testing and evaluating.

## The Balance of Discernment

BALANCING DISCERNMENT is essential. While being cautious, believers should not become overly suspicious of every experience. A healthy approach to recognising influences involves prayer, Scripture, accountability, and a reliance on the Holy Spirit.

**James 1:5:** "But if any of you lacks wisdom, let him ask of God, who gives to all liberally and without reproach; and it will be given to him."

Believers can ask God for wisdom when discerning influences. He is the source of wisdom and will provide it generously.

## Key Takeaways: Recognising Angelic and Demonic Influences

RECOGNISING ANGELIC and demonic influences is vital for believers in the unseen struggle. Key takeaways include:

1. **Discerning Angelic Influences:** Angelic influences bring peace, guidance, messages in line with Scripture, encouragement, and alignment with God's will.

2. **Discerning Demonic Influences:** Demonic influences bring confusion, fear, temptation, deception, discord, division, and contradiction to God's Word.

3. **The Importance of Biblical Discernment:** The Bible is the foundation for discerning influences. Testing them against Scripture is crucial.

4. **Practical Steps for Discernment:** Believers can use prayer, testing against Scripture, seeking accountability, focusing on the fruit, and praying for protection.

5. **Balancing Discernment:** A balanced approach to discernment involves reliance on God's wisdom and the guidance of the Holy Spirit.

As believers continue their journey in the unseen struggle, recognising these influences enables them to navigate the spiritual battlefield with greater wisdom and clarity.

# Spiritual Discernment and Warfare

In the ongoing spiritual battle, spiritual discernment is vital for believers. This section explores the significance of spiritual discernment, its biblical foundations, and its role in the believer's warfare against the unseen forces of darkness.

**1 Corinthians 2:14:** "Now the natural man doesn't receive the things of God's Spirit, for they are foolishness to him, and he can't know them, because they are spiritually discerned."

This verse highlights the necessity of spiritual discernment in comprehending the things of God's Spirit. It distinguishes the natural mindset from the spiritually discerning.

## The Significance of Spiritual Discernment

SPIRITUAL DISCERNMENT holds immense significance for believers:

**1. Recognising Truth from Deception:** In a world filled with spiritual counterfeits and falsehoods, spiritual discernment allows believers to distinguish truth from deception.

**2. Guiding Decision-Making:** Spiritual discernment aids decision-making by seeking God's wisdom and understanding His will.

**3. Identifying Spiritual Influences:** It helps believers identify the sources of spiritual influences, whether from God, angels, or demons.

**4. Protection from Deceptive Spirits:** Discernment safeguards believers from being deceived by false teachings or deceptive spirits.

**5. Strengthening Faith:** Spiritual discernment deepens one's faith by perceiving God's hand in various situations.

**Philippians 1:9-10:** "This I pray, that your love may abound yet more and more in knowledge and all discernment so that you may approve the things that are excellent, that you may be sincere and without offence to the day of Christ."

Paul's prayer for the Philippians emphasises the importance of knowledge and discernment, enabling believers to approve what is excellent and remain blameless until the day of Christ.

## Biblical Foundations of Spiritual Discernment

THE BIBLE PROVIDES strong foundations for the practice of spiritual discernment:

**Proverbs 2:6:** "For Yahweh gives wisdom. Out of his mouth comes knowledge and understanding."

Wisdom and understanding are gifts from God, essential for spiritual discernment. Believers receive these through seeking Him and His Word.

**Hebrews 4:12:** "For the word of God is living, and active, and sharper than any two-edged sword, and piercing even to the dividing of soul and spirit, of both joints and marrow and can discern the thoughts and intentions of the heart."

Hebrews 4:12 highlights the potency of God's Word in discerning the thoughts and intentions of the heart. The Bible is a foundational tool for spiritual discernment.

**1 John 4:1:** "Beloved, don't believe every spirit, but test the spirits, whether they are of God because many false prophets have gone out into the world."

Testing the spirits is crucial to spiritual discernment, as false prophets and deceptive spirits abound.

## The Role of Spiritual Discernment in Warfare

IN THE UNSEEN STRUGGLE, spiritual discernment serves as a powerful weapon:

**1. Recognising Deceptive Influences:** Believers can discern when they are under deceptive influences and resist the enemy's attempts to mislead them.

**2. Identifying God's Guidance:** Discernment helps believers identify when God is leading and guiding them, ensuring they stay aligned with His will.

**3. Praying in Discernment:** Believers can pray for discernment in their spiritual battles, seeking God's wisdom and guidance.

**4. Discerning False Teachings:** Spiritual discernment safeguards against false teachings and heresies that may lead believers astray.

**Matthew 24:24:** "For there will arise false Christs and false prophets, and they will show great signs and wonders, to lead astray, if possible, even the chosen ones."

The words of Jesus in Matthew 24:24 warn about the rise of false teachings and deceptive signs. Spiritual discernment is the key to avoiding being led astray.

## Practical Steps for Developing Spiritual Discernment

DEVELOPING SPIRITUAL discernment requires active effort and reliance on God:

**1. Pray for Discernment:** Begin by asking God for discernment in all areas of life, including spiritual battles.

**2. Study God's Word:** Regularly study and meditate on the Bible. It is the primary source of spiritual wisdom and discernment.

**3. Seek Accountability:** Share your experiences and concerns with fellow believers or spiritual mentors who can provide guidance.

**4. Test the Spirits:** Continuously test spiritual influences and teachings against God's Word to ensure they align with the truth.

**5. Listen to the Holy Spirit:** Be attentive to the promptings and guidance of the Holy Spirit in your life.

**James 1:5:** "But if any of you lacks wisdom, let him ask of God, who gives to all liberally and without reproach; and it will be given to him."

James encourages believers to ask God for wisdom. God is willing to provide wisdom to those who seek it with a sincere heart.

## The Balance of Spiritual Discernment

WHILE SPIRITUAL DISCERNMENT is crucial, it must be balanced with love and humility. It should not lead to judgment or condemnation of others but to a deeper understanding of God's will.

**Philippians 1:9:** "This I pray, that your love may abound yet more and more in knowledge and all discernment."

Paul's prayer for the Philippians emphasises the necessity of love alongside knowledge and discernment. Love is the context in which discernment should operate.

## Key Takeaways: Spiritual Discernment and Warfare

SPIRITUAL DISCERNMENT is vital in the believer's spiritual warfare. Key takeaways regarding spiritual discernment include:

1. **Significance of Spiritual Discernment:** It helps believers recognise truth from deception, guides decision-making, identifies spiritual influences, protects from deceptive spirits, and strengthens faith.
2. **Biblical Foundations:** The Bible is the primary source for spiritual discernment, offering wisdom and understanding.
3. **Role in Warfare:** Spiritual discernment is essential for recognising deceptive influences, identifying God's guidance, praying in discernment, and discerning false teachings.
4. **Practical Steps for Development:** Steps for developing discernment include prayer, studying God's Word, seeking accountability, testing the spirits, and listening to the Holy Spirit.
5. **The Balance of Discernment:** Discernment should be balanced with love and humility, leading to a deeper understanding of God's will and not judgment.

As believers continue to engage in the unseen struggle against spiritual forces, spiritual discernment becomes an invaluable asset, enabling them to navigate the battlefield with wisdom and clarity.

# Strategies for Fending Off Demonic Oppression

In the ongoing spiritual battle, believers may encounter demonic oppression. It's crucial to understand the strategies for fending off such oppression, relying on God's Word and spiritual weapons. This section explores these strategies and their biblical foundations.

**1 Peter 5:8:** "Be sober and self-controlled. Be watchful. Your adversary, the devil, walks around like a roaring lion, seeking whom he may devour."

This verse serves as a sobering reminder of the adversary's intent to harm believers. Fending off demonic oppression is an essential part of the Christian's spiritual journey.

## The Significance of Fending Off Demonic Oppression

FENDING OFF DEMONIC oppression is significant for several reasons:

**1. Protecting One's Faith:** Demonic oppression can weaken a believer's faith and hinder spiritual growth. Fending it off is essential for maintaining a strong faith.

**2. Ensuring Mental and Emotional Well-being:** Oppression can manifest as mental and emotional anguish. Fending it off is crucial for one's mental and emotional health.

**3. Resisting Spiritual Attacks:** Demonic oppression is a form of spiritual attack. Fending it off is necessary for continued spiritual growth and stability.

**4. Maintaining Godly Influence:** Believers must resist oppression to continue being godly influences in their families, communities, and the world.

**2 Corinthians 2:11:** "That no advantage may be gained over us by Satan, for we are not ignorant of his schemes."

Understanding the schemes of the enemy is crucial for fending off demonic oppression. Believers should not be ignorant of Satan's tactics.

## Biblical Foundations of Fending Off Demonic Oppression

THE BIBLE PROVIDES a strong foundation for strategies to fend off demonic oppression:

**James 4:7:** "Be subject therefore to God. But resist the devil, and he will flee from you."

James instructs believers to submit to God and resist the devil. This biblical principle is central to fending off demonic oppression.

**Ephesians 6:10-11:** "Finally, be strong in the Lord, and in the strength of his might. Put on the armour of God, that you may be able to stand against the devil's wiles."

Ephesians 6:10-11 emphasises the need to be strong in the Lord and put on God's full armour. This armour equips believers to stand against the devil's cunning schemes.

**1 John 4:4:** "You are of God, little children, and have overcome them; because greater is he who is in you than he who is in the world."

This verse reassures believers that they have overcome the world and its demonic forces because the One in them is greater than the One in the world.

## Strategies for Fending Off Demonic Oppression

BELIEVERS CAN EMPLOY various strategies to fend off demonic oppression:

**1. Prayer:** Prayer is a powerful weapon against demonic oppression. Seek God's protection, guidance, and deliverance through prayer.

**2. Scripture:** Use God's Word as a defensive weapon. The Bible is likened to a sword in the spiritual armour (Ephesians 6:17) and effectively repels the enemy.

**3. Submission to God:** Submit to God and His authority. Resist the devil's influence, knowing he must flee (James 4:7).

**4. Worship and Praise:** Engage in worship and praise to shift the atmosphere and invite God's presence, which repels darkness.

**5. Fasting:** Fasting can be a powerful spiritual discipline to break the bonds of oppression and seek God's intervention.

**6. Seeking Accountability:** Share your struggles with fellow believers or a trusted spiritual mentor. They can provide support and prayer.

**7. Renouncing Sin:** Confess and repent of any known sin. Sin can open doors to demonic influence.

**1 Peter 5:9:** "Withstand him, steadfast in your faith, knowing that your brothers in the world are undergoing the same sufferings."

Believers are encouraged to withstand the devil, remaining steadfast in their faith. This resistance is grounded in the knowledge that fellow believers share similar experiences.

## The Role of the Holy Spirit in Fending Off Demonic Oppression

THE HOLY SPIRIT PLAYS a significant role in fending off demonic oppression:

**1. Conviction of Sin:** The Holy Spirit convicts believers of sin, prompting them to repent and close the doors to demonic influence.

**2. Discernment:** The Spirit provides discernment to recognise the enemy's schemes and respond appropriately.

**3. Empowerment:** Believers can draw on the Holy Spirit's empowerment to resist the devil and stand firm in their faith.

**4. Comfort:** The Holy Spirit offers comfort and assurance in moments of oppression.

**5. Prayer:** The Spirit intercedes for believers in times of weakness and oppression, helping them pray effectively.

**Romans 8:26-27:** "In the same way, the Spirit also helps our weaknesses, for we don't know how to pray as we ought. But the Spirit makes intercession for us with groanings that can't be uttered. He who searches the hearts knows what is on the Spirit's mind because he makes intercession for the saints according to God."

These verses from Romans highlight the Holy Spirit's role in helping believers during their weaknesses, including times of spiritual oppression. The Spirit aids in prayer and intercession, providing comfort and strength in battles.

## The Importance of Perseverance

PERSEVERANCE IS VITAL when fending off demonic oppression. Oppression can be prolonged and challenging, but believers must stand firm in their faith.

**Galatians 6:9:** "Let us not be weary in doing good, for we will reap in due season if we don't give up."

Believers are encouraged not to grow weary in doing good, knowing there will be a harvest if they do not give up. This applies to resisting demonic oppression and standing strong in faith.

**1 Peter 1:6-7:** "Wherein you greatly rejoice, though now for a little while, if need be, you have been put to grief in various trials, that the proof of your faith, which is more precious than gold that perishes even though it is tested by fire, may be found to result in praise, glory, and honour at the revelation of Jesus Christ."

Trials and testing, including the battle against oppression, serve to refine one's faith. Believers must understand that enduring these trials leads to praise, glory, and honour when Christ is revealed.

## Seeking Professional Help

IN SEVERE OR PROLONGED oppression, seeking professional help, including medical, psychological, or pastoral support, is important. Demonic oppression can manifest in ways that impact mental and emotional well-being, and seeking assistance is a responsible and biblical course of action.

**Proverbs 15:22:** "Where there is no counsel, plans fail; but in a multitude of counsellors they are established."

Proverbs emphasise the importance of seeking counsel. In situations of oppression, many counsellors can help establish a path toward deliverance and healing.

## Key Takeaways: Strategies for Fending Off Demonic Oppression

TO SUMMARISE, STRATEGIES for fending off demonic oppression are crucial in the believer's journey through the unseen struggle. Key takeaways regarding these strategies include:

1. **Significance of Fending Off Demonic Oppression:** It protects one's faith, mental and emotional well-being, resistance against spiritual attacks, and ability to be a godly influence.
2. **Biblical Foundations:** The Bible emphasises the importance of submitting to God, putting on the whole armour of God, and resisting the devil.
3. **Strategies for Fending Off Demonic Oppression:** Believers can employ prayer, Scripture, submission to God, worship and praise, fasting, seeking accountability, renouncing sin, and seeking professional help when necessary.
4. **The Role of the Holy Spirit:** The Holy Spirit is crucial in offering conviction, discernment, empowerment, comfort, and intercession in times of oppression.
5. **The Importance of Perseverance:** Believers must persevere in their faith when battling oppression, understanding that trials refine and strengthen their faith.
6. **Seeking Professional Help:** When oppression is severe or

prolonged and affects mental or emotional well-being, seeking professional assistance is a responsible action.

In the face of spiritual battles and demonic oppression, believers are equipped with a spiritual arsenal rooted in God's Word and empowered by the Holy Spirit. These strategies are essential for fending oppression, standing firm in faith, and serving as lights in a dark world.

# Navigating the Spiritual Battle as a Believer

As believers engage in the spiritual battle, they must navigate the challenges and victories that come with it. This section explores the journey of navigating the spiritual battle, drawing insights from the Bible and providing guidance for believers.

**1 Corinthians 15:57:** "But thanks be to God, who gives us the victory through our Lord Jesus Christ."

This verse reminds believers that victory is attainable through Jesus Christ, even amid the spiritual battle.

## The Spiritual Battle's Reality

THE FIRST STEP IN NAVIGATING the spiritual battle is acknowledging its reality. This battle is not metaphorical but a spiritual struggle against unseen forces.

**Ephesians 6:12:** "For our wrestling is not against flesh and blood, but against the principalities, against the powers, against the world's rulers of the darkness of this age, and against the spiritual forces of wickedness in the heavenly places."

Ephesians 6:12 clarifies that the battle is against spiritual forces of wickedness. Understanding this truth is the foundation for navigating the spiritual battle.

## The Whole Armour of God

EPHESIANS 6:13-18 OUTLINES the "whole armour of God," which is indispensable for believers in the spiritual battle. Each piece of this armour plays a crucial role:

**1. The Belt of Truth (Ephesians 6:14):** Truth holds the believer's spiritual armour together. It means living in honesty and integrity, firmly rooted in God's Word.

**2. The Breastplate of Righteousness (Ephesians 6:14):** Righteousness protects the heart and signifies a life of moral integrity and obedience to God.

**3. The Shoes of the Gospel of Peace (Ephesians 6:15):** These shoes enable believers to move with the message of peace, ready to share the Gospel and stand firm.

**4. The Shield of Faith (Ephesians 6:16):** Faith is the shield against the enemy's attacks. Believers trust God's promises and rely on His power.

**5. The Helmet of Salvation (Ephesians 6:17):** The helmet guards the believer's mind, assuring the assurance of salvation.

**6. The Sword of the Spirit (Ephesians 6:17):** The Word of God is the believer's offensive weapon, enabling them to counter the enemy's lies with the truth.

**7. Prayer (Ephesians 6:18):** Prayer is not just a piece of armour but an essential part of using the whole armour effectively. The believer constantly communicates with God, seeking guidance, strength, and deliverance.

## The Role of Faith in Navigating the Battle

FAITH IS A CENTRAL element in the believer's journey through the spiritual battle. It's through faith that believers overcome challenges and obstacles.

**1 John 5:4:** "For whatever is born of God overcomes the world. This is the victory that has overcome the world: your faith."

This verse highlights the significance of faith in overcoming the world. Faith births the victory that believers need in navigating the spiritual battle.

**Hebrews 11:6:** "Without faith, it is impossible to be well pleasing to him, for he who comes to God must believe that he exists and that he is a rewarder of those who seek him."

Hebrews emphasises that faith is essential in seeking God. Believers must believe in God's existence and willingness to reward those diligently seeking Him.

## The Power of Prayer in Navigating the Battle

PRAYER IS A POWERFUL tool in the believer's arsenal for navigating the spiritual battle. Through prayer, believers connect with God, seek His guidance, and find strength.

**Ephesians 6:18:** "With all prayer and requests, praying at all times in the Spirit, and being watchful to this end in all perseverance and requests for all the saints."

This verse encourages believers to pray continually, be watchful, and persevere in their requests. Prayer should be a constant and ongoing practice that is not limited to specific times.

**James 5:16:** "Confess your offences to one another and pray for one another, that you may be healed. The insistent prayer of a righteous person is powerfully effective."

James stresses the effectiveness of prayer, particularly the prayer of a righteous person. Confession and intercession are powerful components of prayer.

## Overcoming Fear in the Battle

FEAR IS A COMMON EMOTION in the spiritual battle. The enemy often tries to instil fear in believers, but God provides the means to overcome it.

**2 Timothy 1:7:** "For God didn't give us a spirit of fear but of power, love, and self-control."

This verse from 2 Timothy reminds believers that God has equipped them with a spirit of power, love, and self-control rather than fear. Replacing fear with trust in God's strength and love is essential in navigating the spiritual battle.

**1 John 4:18:** "There is no fear in love, but perfect love casts out fear because fear has punishment. He who fears is not made perfect in love."

This verse emphasises that perfect love casts out fear. Believers can find solace in God's perfect love, trusting that it drives away fear and the associated punishment.

## Perseverance in the Battle

NAVIGATING THE SPIRITUAL battle requires perseverance. Challenges will arise, but believers must remain steadfast in their faith and commitment to God.

**Galatians 6:9:** "Let us not be weary in doing good, for we will reap in due season if we don't give up."

Galatians reminds believers not to grow weary in doing good, assuring them that they will reap in due season if they do not give up. Perseverance is key to victory.

**James 1:12:** "Blessed is the man who endures temptation, for when he has been approved, he will receive the crown of life, which the Lord promised to those who love him."

Endurance and perseverance in the face of temptation lead to a crown of life, a promise for those who love the Lord. Navigating the spiritual battle is a test of endurance, ultimately leading to a blessed reward.

## Fellowship and Support

NAVIGATING THE SPIRITUAL battle is not a solitary journey. Fellowship and support from other believers are essential.

**Ecclesiastes 4:9-10:** "Two are better than one because they have a good reward for their labour. If they fall, the one will lift up his fellow, but woe to him who is alone when he falls and doesn't have another to help him up."

Ecclesiastes emphasises the importance of having support and companionship. Believers can help one another when facing challenges in the spiritual battle.

**Hebrews 10:24-25:** "Let us consider how to provoke one another to love and good works, not forsaking our own assembling together, as the custom of some is, but exhorting one another, and so much the more, as you see the Day approaching."

Hebrews encourages believers to gather together, exhort one another, and provoke love and good works. This fellowship strengthens the body of Christ and helps believers navigate the spiritual battle.

## Victorious Living

WHILE NAVIGATING THE spiritual battle involves challenges, it also offers opportunities for victorious living.

**Romans 8:37:** "No, in all these things, we are more than conquerors through him who loved us."

This verse in Romans declares that believers are more than conquerors through the love of Christ. In the spiritual battle, victory is not merely surviving but thriving in faith.

**1 Corinthians 15:57:** "But thanks be to God, who gives us the victory through our Lord Jesus Christ."

As believers navigate the spiritual battle, they can be assured of victory, not through their own strength, but through the power of Christ.

. . . .

THE SPIRITUAL BATTLE is a reality for believers, and navigating it with the right tools and mindset is essential. The whole armour of God, faith, prayer, and perseverance are crucial elements in this journey. Overcoming fear, staying connected in fellowship, and living victoriously are all part of the believer's path through the spiritual battle. By anchoring their faith in God and trusting in His promises, believers can confidently navigate the unseen struggle, knowing that victory is ultimately theirs.

# Chapter 8: Conclusion

In this comprehensive exploration of the spiritual battle, the presence of angels, demons, and the believer's need for the whole armour of God, we have explored the biblical perspective on these subjects. It's crucial to summarise the key points to reinforce understanding of these profound spiritual concepts.

## 1. The Spiritual Battle

**EPHESIANS 6:12:** "For our wrestling is not against flesh and blood, but against the principalities, against the powers, against the world's rulers of the darkness of this age, and against the spiritual forces of wickedness in the heavenly places."

The spiritual battle is a reality, and believers must acknowledge its existence. It is not a battle against flesh and blood but against spiritual forces of wickedness in the heavenly places.

## 2. The Whole Armour of God

**EPHESIANS 6:13-18:** "Therefore, put on the whole armour of God, that you may be able to withstand in the evil day, and, having done all, to stand. Stand therefore, having the utility belt of truth buckled around your waist, and having put on the breastplate of righteousness, and having fitted your feet with the preparation of the gospel of peace; above all, taking up the shield of faith, with which you will be able to quench all the fiery darts of the evil one. Take the helmet of salvation, and the sword of the Spirit, which is the word of God; with all prayer and requests, praying at all times in the Spirit, and being watchful to this end in all perseverance and requests for all the saints."

The whole armour of God is indispensable for believers in the spiritual battle. Each piece of this armour is crucial in protection, defence, and empowerment. It includes the belt of truth, the breastplate of righteousness, the shoes of the gospel of peace, the shield of faith, the helmet of salvation, the sword of the Spirit, and prayer.

## 3. The Nature of Angels

**HEBREWS 1:14:** "Aren't they all serving spirits, sent out to do service for the sake of those who will inherit salvation?"

Angels are heavenly beings created by God to serve and minister to those who will inherit salvation. They are messengers of God and play various roles in God's divine plan.

## 4. Angelic Appearances in the Old Testament

IN THE OLD TESTAMENT, angels appeared to individuals like Abraham, Jacob, Moses, and Daniel. They delivered messages, provided guidance, and protected God's chosen people. These appearances reveal the significant role of angels in God's plan throughout history.

## 5. Angelic Appearances in the New Testament

IN THE NEW TESTAMENT, angels played a pivotal role in the birth of Jesus, announcing His arrival to shepherds and providing guidance to Joseph and Mary. They also appeared to the disciples in the empty tomb, confirming Jesus' resurrection.

## 6. The Role of Angels in Biblical Narratives

ANGELS SERVE AS MESSENGERS, protectors, guides, and worshippers of God. They play vital roles in biblical narratives, aiding individuals and nations in fulfilling God's plan. They also engage in spiritual warfare against demonic forces.

## 7. The Nature of Demons

**MATTHEW 8:28-29:** "When he came to the other side, into the country of the Gergesenes, two people possessed by demons met him there, coming out of the tombs, exceedingly fierce, so that nobody could pass that way. Behold, they cried out, saying, 'What do we have to do with you, Jesus, Son of God? Have you come here to torment us before the time?'"

Demons are malevolent, unclean spirits that seek to harm and possess individuals. They recognise Jesus as the Son of God and fear His power.

## 8. Demonic Influences in the Old Testament

IN THE OLD TESTAMENT, instances of demonic influence are evident, such as the story of Saul and the spirit of distress from the Lord. These accounts highlight the reality of demonic forces and their influence on humanity.

## 9. Demonic Influences in the New Testament

THE NEW TESTAMENT PORTRAYS several accounts of demonic possessions and Jesus' authority over demons. It emphasises the ongoing battle against demonic forces during Jesus and the early church.

## 10. The Role of Demons in Biblical Narratives

DEMONS ATTEMPT TO THWART God's plan and oppress individuals. They recognise Jesus as a threat to their existence and seek to torment and possess human beings. However, the power of Christ prevails, and demons are cast out.

## 11. The Biblical Command to Worship God Alone

**EXODUS 20:3:** "You shall have no other gods before me."

The Bible emphasises the exclusive worship of God. Believers are commanded to worship and serve God alone, as any other form of worship is considered idolatry.

## 12. The Pitfalls of Angel Worship

**COLOSSIANS 2:18:** "Let no one rob you of your prize by a voluntary humility and worshipping of the angels, dwelling in the things which he has not seen, vainly puffed up by his fleshly mind."

The Bible warns against the worship of angels, as it can lead to deception and distract believers from the true object of worship, which is God.

## 13. The Consequences of Misplaced Devotion

MISPLACED DEVOTION, such as angel worship or idolatry, has consequences. It can lead to spiritual deception, hinder the believer's relationship with God, and open the door to demonic influences.

## 14. The Cosmic Battle Between Angels and Demons

**REVELATION 12:7:** "There was war in the sky. Michael and his angels made war on the dragon. The dragon and his angels made war."

Revelation portrays a cosmic battle between the archangel Michael and his angels and the dragon (Satan) and his angels. This spiritual warfare emphasises the ongoing struggle between angels and demons.

## 15. How the Spiritual Realm Affects Our World

THE SPIRITUAL REALM directly impacts the physical world. The actions and interactions of angels and demons have real-world consequences, affecting individuals and nations.

## 16. The Believer's Role in the Spiritual War

BELIEVERS ARE ACTIVE participants in the spiritual war. They are called to resist the devil, put on the whole armour of God, and engage in prayer and spiritual warfare.

## 17. Strategies for Fending Off Demonic Oppression

**JAMES 4:7:** "Be subject therefore to God. But resist the devil, and he will flee from you."

Believers can employ strategies like prayer, Scripture, submission to God, worship and praise, fasting, seeking accountability, renouncing sin, and seeking professional help when facing demonic oppression.

## 18. The Role of the Holy Spirit in Fending Off Demonic Oppression

THE HOLY SPIRIT PROVIDES conviction of sin, discernment, empowerment, comfort, and intercession in the battle against demonic oppression.

## 19. Navigating the Spiritual Battle

NAVIGATING THE SPIRITUAL battle requires acknowledging its reality, putting on the whole armour of God, having faith, engaging in prayer, overcoming fear, persevering in the battle, seeking fellowship and support, and ultimately striving for victorious living.

## 20. How to Recognise Angelic and Demonic Influences

BELIEVERS SHOULD BE discerning in recognising the signs of angelic or demonic influences in their lives and the world around them. This discernment is guided by the Holy Spirit and God's Word.

## 21. Spiritual Discernment and Warfare

SPIRITUAL DISCERNMENT is crucial in identifying spiritual influences and making informed decisions in the battle. Believers are engaged in spiritual warfare and should be vigilant against the schemes of the enemy.

## 22. Strategies for Fending Off Demonic Oppression

BELIEVERS CAN ACCESS various strategies for fending demonic oppression, including prayer, Scripture, submission to God, worship, seeking accountability, renouncing sin, and seeking professional help when necessary.

## 23. The Power of Faith and Prayer

FAITH AND PRAYER ARE powerful tools in the believer's journey through the spiritual battle. Faith enables believers to overcome fear and trust in God's strength, while prayer connects them with God's guidance and strength.

## 24. Overcoming Fear and Persevering

FEAR IS COMMON IN THE spiritual battle, but believers can overcome it by trusting God's perfect love. Perseverance is essential, as it leads to a victorious life.

## 25. The Importance of Fellowship and Support

BELIEVERS SHOULD NOT navigate the spiritual battle alone. Fellowship and support from other believers are essential for encouragement and strength.

## 26. Victorious Living

BELIEVERS ARE MORE than conquerors through Christ; they can live victoriously in the spiritual battle. Victory comes through faith, the whole armour of God, and reliance on God's power.

In conclusion, the spiritual battle is an unseen struggle that permeates the lives of believers. It involves the presence of angels and demons, the need for the whole armour of God, and the believer's active role in navigating this battle. The Bible provides the foundation for understanding these spiritual concepts, and the key points outlined here serve as a comprehensive guide for believers to engage effectively in this ongoing struggle. It is a battle where God's sovereignty has already determined the outcome. Believers can have confidence that they are on the winning side as they stand firm in their faith, put on the whole armour of God, and trust in the power of Christ.

# Encouragement and Warnings

As we conclude our exploration of the spiritual battle, it is essential to encourage and warn believers. This section will draw from biblical passages to offer motivation, hope, and caution to those engaged in the unseen struggle.

## 1. Encouragement in the Spiritual Battle

**ISAIAH 41:10:** "Don't you be afraid, for I am with you. Don't be dismayed, for I am your God. I will strengthen you. Yes, I will help you. Yes, I will uphold you with the right hand of my righteousness."

This verse from Isaiah offers powerful encouragement to believers. It reminds them that God is with them, strengthening and upholding them. In the spiritual battle, when fear or doubt may creep in, believers can find solace in God's promise of His presence and support.

## 2. The Assurance of Victory

**1 CORINTHIANS 15:57:** "But thanks be to God, who gives us the victory through our Lord Jesus Christ."

This verse emphasises the assurance of victory for believers through Jesus Christ. Knowing that God grants victory provides hope and confidence in the spiritual battle.

## 3. The Power of Prayer

**PHILIPPIANS 4:6-7:** "In nothing be anxious, but in everything, by prayer and petition with thanksgiving, let your requests be made known to God. And the peace of God, which surpasses all understanding, will guard your hearts and thoughts in Christ Jesus."

Believers can find encouragement in the power of prayer. When facing challenges in the spiritual battle, praying to God brings His peace that surpasses understanding. This peace guards hearts and minds, offering reassurance in times of turmoil.

## 4. The Role of the Holy Spirit

**ROMANS 8:26:** "In the same way, the Spirit also helps our weaknesses, for we don't know how to pray as we ought. But the Spirit himself makes intercession for us with groanings which can't be uttered."

The Holy Spirit's role as our Helper is a source of encouragement. When we encounter challenges or uncertainty in the spiritual battle, the Spirit aids us in our weaknesses, even when we don't know how to pray. This assurance of the Spirit's intercession provides comfort and confidence.

## 5. Perseverance and Endurance

**JAMES 1:12:** "Blessed is the man who endures temptation, for when he has been approved, he will receive the crown of life, which the Lord promised to those who love him."

Endurance in the spiritual battle leads to a crown of life, a promise to those who love the Lord. This encouragement reminds believers that perseverance in facing challenges is rewarded with a blessed future.

## 6. The Support of Fellow Believers

**GALATIANS 6:2:** "Bear one another's burdens, and so fulfil the law of Christ."

Encouragement often comes through the support of fellow believers. Bearing one another's burdens and walking together in faith is essential to the Christian journey. In the spiritual battle, believers should seek and offer support within the body of Christ.

## 7. Warning Against Complacency

**1 CORINTHIANS 10:12:** "Therefore, let him who thinks he stands be careful that he doesn't fall."

This warning from 1 Corinthians reminds believers not to become complacent in their faith. In the spiritual battle, overconfidence can lead to stumbling. It's crucial to remain vigilant and humble, recognising our dependence on God.

## 8. The Danger of Idolatry

**1 JOHN 5:21:** "Little children, keep yourselves from idols."

Believers are cautioned against idolatry. In the spiritual battle, the temptation to worship or place undue importance on anything other than God is a significant danger. This warning emphasises the need for exclusive devotion to the Almighty.

## 9. The Deception of False Spirits

**1 JOHN 4:1:** "Beloved, don't believe every spirit, but test the spirits, whether they are of God because many false prophets have gone out into the world."

Believers are cautioned not to believe every spirit but to test them to discern whether they are of God. The spiritual battle involves the presence of false spirits and deceptive influences, necessitating discernment and caution.

## 10. The Consequences of Disobedience

**1 SAMUEL 15:23:** "For rebellion is the sin of witchcraft, and stubbornness is idolatry and teraphim. Because you have rejected the Lord's word, he has also rejected you from being king."

The consequences of disobedience are highlighted in this warning from 1 Samuel. Disobedience, rebellion, and stubbornness can have severe consequences. Believers are reminded that in the spiritual battle, choosing disobedience over obedience can lead to estrangement from God.

## 11. The Battle is Ongoing

**1 PETER 5:8:** "Be sober and self-controlled. Be watchful. Your adversary, the devil, walks around like a roaring lion, seeking whom he may devour."

This verse from 1 Peter reminds believers that the spiritual battle is ongoing. The adversary, the devil, continually seeks to devour those who are not watchful. This warning emphasises the need for vigilance and readiness.

## 12. Guarding Your Heart and Mind

**PROVERBS 4:23:** "Keep your heart with all diligence, for out of it is the wellspring of life."

Believers are encouraged to guard their hearts diligently. In the spiritual battle, the heart and mind are vulnerable to various influences. Protecting them is vital for maintaining a strong and steadfast faith.

## 13. The Spiritual Battle Is Real

**EPHESIANS 6:12:** "For our wrestling is not against flesh and blood, but against the principalities, against the powers, against the world's rulers of the darkness of this age, and against the spiritual forces of wickedness in the heavenly places."

The reality of the spiritual battle is a recurring theme in Scripture. Believers are encouraged to understand that this battle is not a metaphor but a genuine struggle against spiritual forces. Awareness of this reality is the first step in preparing for it.

## 14. The Importance of Faith in Christ

**1 JOHN 5:4:** "For whatever is born of God overcomes the world. This is the victory that has overcome the world: your faith."

Victory in the spiritual battle comes through faith in Christ. Believers should anchor their trust in Him, recognising that their faith is the key to overcoming their challenges.

## 15. The Role of the Word of God

**HEBREWS 4:12:** "For the word of God is living, and active, and sharper than any two-edged sword, and piercing even to the dividing of soul and spirit, of both joints and marrow and can discern the thoughts and intentions of the heart."

The Word of God is a powerful weapon in the spiritual battle. It is living, active, and sharp, discerning the thoughts and intentions of the heart. Believers are encouraged to immerse themselves in the Word, allowing it to guide and protect them.

## 16. The Hope of Eternity

**2 CORINTHIANS 4:17-18:** "For our light affliction, which is for the moment, works for us more and more exceedingly an eternal weight of glory, while we don't look at the things which are seen, but at the things which are not seen. For the things which are seen are temporal, but the things which are not seen are eternal."

In the spiritual battle, this passage from 2 Corinthians offers hope. Believers are reminded that their difficulties are temporary and light compared to the eternal glory that awaits them. This perspective can provide encouragement and endurance in the battle.

• • • •

IN THE UNSEEN STRUGGLE of the spiritual battle, believers are equipped with encouragement and warnings from the Word of God.

These assurances and cautions guide navigating the challenges, dangers, and victories that come with the territory. It is a journey where faith, the whole armour of God, prayer, discernment, perseverance, and reliance on the Holy Spirit are essential. By heeding these encouragements and warnings, believers can stand firm, overcome, and ultimately experience the triumph promised in Christ.

# Looking Ahead: Your Role in the Battle

As we conclude this journey through the spiritual battle, we must consider each believer's role in this ongoing struggle. The Bible offers guidance, and through the Word of God, we can find direction and purpose in the battle.

## 1. Your Identity in Christ

**2 CORINTHIANS 5:17 (WEB):** "Therefore if anyone is in Christ, he is a new creation. The old things have passed away. Behold, all things have become new."

Your identity in Christ is the foundation of your role in the spiritual battle. You became a new creation when you accepted Christ as your Lord and Savior. This new identity equips you with the power of the Holy Spirit, making you a participant in the battle.

## 2. Be Strong in the Lord

**EPHESIANS 6:10:** "Finally, be strong in the Lord, and in the strength of his might."

Your role in the battle begins with being strong in the Lord. This strength is not self-generated but comes from your reliance on God's might. It's an acknowledgement that you cannot navigate the battle in your own power but through His.

## 3. Put on the Whole Armour of God

**EPHESIANS 6:11:** "Put on the whole armour of God, that you may be able to stand against the wiles of the devil."

Your role involves actively putting on the whole armour of God. This is not a passive act but a deliberate choice to clothe yourself with truth, righteousness, the gospel of peace, faith, salvation, and the Word of God. This armour equips you to stand against the schemes of the devil.

## 4. Stand Firm

**EPHESIANS 6:13:** "Therefore, put on the whole armour of God, that you may be able to withstand in the evil day, and, having done all, to stand."

Your role in the battle includes standing firm. This is not a call to be aggressive but resolute in your faith, anchored in the truth of God's Word. It's a reminder that as a believer, you are not meant to be tossed about by the challenges of the spiritual battle but to stand in God's strength.

## 5. The Power of Prayer

**EPHESIANS 6:18:** "With all prayer and requests, praying at all times in the Spirit, and being watchful to this end in all perseverance and requests for all the saints."

Your role in the battle includes the power of prayer. Prayer is not merely a religious exercise but a potent weapon. It connects you with God's guidance and strength, empowers you to intercede for others, and keeps you watchful in the battle.

## 6. Resist the Devil

**JAMES 4:7:** "Be subject therefore to God. But resist the devil, and he will flee from you."

Your role involves resisting the devil. While the devil is a formidable adversary, you have the authority in Christ to resist his schemes. This resistance is an active choice to stand against the enemy's influence.

## 7. Walk in Love and Unity

**EPHESIANS 4:2-3:** "With all lowliness and humility, with patience, bearing with one another in love; being eager to keep the unity of the Spirit in the bond of peace."

Your role in the battle extends to your relationships with fellow believers. Walking in love and unity is essential. Divisions and strife among believers weaken the body of Christ. Still, unity strengthens it, making it more resilient in the spiritual battle.

## 8. Be Discerning

**1 JOHN 4:1:** "Beloved, don't believe every spirit, but test the spirits, whether they are of God because many false prophets have gone out into the world."

Your role involves discernment. As a believer, you are called to test the spirits and discern whether they are of God. This discernment protects you from deception and false influences in the spiritual battle.

## 9. Seek Accountability and Fellowship

**GALATIANS 6:2:** "Bear one another's burdens, and so fulfil the law of Christ."

Your role in the battle includes seeking accountability and fellowship. Believers are not meant to navigate the spiritual battle alone. Bearing one another's burdens and walking together in faith is essential for encouragement and strength.

## 10. Pursue Holiness

**1 PETER 1:16:** "Because it is written, 'You shall be holy, for I am holy.'"

Your role in the battle involves pursuing holiness. Holiness is not a legalistic standard but a reflection of God's character. Honouring God and resisting the enemy's attempts to draw you away from Him is a commitment.

## 11. Stand in Righteousness

**EPHESIANS 6:14**: "Stand therefore, having the utility belt of truth buckled around your waist, and putting on the breastplate of righteousness."

Your role in the battle includes standing in righteousness. Just as the breastplate guards the vital organs, righteousness guards your heart and moral standing. It's a commitment to living righteously and resisting the enemy's attempts to lead you into sin.

## 12. Engage in the Battle for Souls

**MATTHEW 28:19-20:** "Go, and make disciples of all nations, baptising them in the name of the Father and the Son and of the Holy Spirit, teaching them to observe all things that I commanded you."

Your role involves actively engaging in the battle for souls. The Great Commission given by Jesus calls believers to share the gospel and make disciples. This is a critical aspect of the spiritual battle, as it rescues souls from the dominion of darkness.

## 13. Renew Your Mind

**ROMANS 12:2:** "Don't be conformed to this world, but be transformed by the renewing of your mind, so that you may prove what is the good, well-pleasing, and perfect will of God."

Your role includes renewing your mind. In the battle, your thoughts and beliefs are battlegrounds. Renewing your mind through the Word of God is essential to discerning and living in God's will.

## 14. Overcome Evil with Good

**ROMANS 12:21:** "Don't be overcome by evil, but overcome evil with good."

Your role in the battle is to overcome evil with good. In a world filled with darkness and conflict, believers are called to respond with love, kindness, and good deeds, demonstrating the transformative power of Christ.

## 15. Be a Light in the Darkness

**MATTHEW 5:14:** "You are the light of the world. A city located on a hill can't be hidden."

Your role involves being a light in the darkness. As a believer, you are a beacon of hope and truth in a world that often dwells in spiritual obscurity. Your actions, words, and character can lead others to Christ.

## 16. Remember Your Eternal Perspective

**2 CORINTHIANS 4:18:** "While we don't look at the things which are seen, but at the things which are not seen. For the things which are seen are temporal, but the things which are not seen are eternal."

Your role in the battle includes keeping an eternal perspective. Remember that the challenges and trials you face are temporary. Still, the rewards and glory that await you in eternity are eternal. This perspective can provide hope and endurance in the battle.

• • • •

THE SPIRITUAL BATTLE is ongoing, and your role in it is significant. It is a battle that requires strength in the Lord, the whole armour of God, prayer, discernment, unity, holiness, and a commitment to engaging in the battle for souls. As you walk in the truth of God's Word, standing firm in righteousness and resisting the enemy, you become a vital part of the larger spiritual warfare. Your actions and choices impact not only your own spiritual journey but also the lives of those around you. In the unseen struggle, you reflect Christ's love, truth, and hope to a world needing His redeeming grace.

# Questions for Reflection

Questions on Angels and Demons:

1. What are the Seraphim, and what is their primary role?
2. What is the significance of Cherubim in the Bible?
3. What is the role of angels in biblical narratives?
4. Who is the "Prince of Demons" in the New Testament?
5. In what way did angels play a role in the birth of Jesus?

**Questions on Spiritual Warfare:**

1. What is the whole armour of God, and why is it important in spiritual warfare?
2. How did Jesus respond to Satan's temptations in the wilderness?
3. What are some strategies for believers to fend off demonic oppression?
4. How does spiritual discernment help believers in the unseen struggle
5. What is the ultimate source of believers' strength in spiritual warfare?

**Questions on the Cosmic Battle:**

1. How does the cosmic battle between angels and demons impact the physical world?
2. In what ways can believers be a light in the darkness?
3. What is the importance of keeping an eternal perspective in the spiritual war?
4. How does the unseen struggle reflect the ongoing battle for souls?

## Questions on the Armor of God:

1. What is the purpose of the belt of truth in the whole armour of God?
2. How does the breastplate of righteousness protect believers in the spiritual battle?
3. What is the role of the shoes of the gospel of peace in the whole armour of God?
4. How does the shield of faith help believers fend off the devil's attacks?
5. What is the significance of the helmet of salvation in spiritual warfare?
6. How does the sword of the Spirit differ from other pieces of the armour of God?

## Questions on Spiritual Discernment:

1. What is the role of spiritual discernment in recognising angelic and demonic influences?
2. How can believers cultivate spiritual discernment in their lives?
3. Why is spiritual discernment important for believers in the unseen struggle?
4. What are the key signs of demonic oppression, and how can believers discern them?

## Questions on Looking Ahead:

1. How can believers actively engage in the battle for souls?
2. What role does renewing the mind play in the believer's spiritual journey?
3. How can believers overcome evil with good, and why is this important in the spiritual battle?

4. How can believers maintain an eternal perspective in the spiritual battle?

# Questions on Angels and Demons:

1. Q: What are the Seraphim, and what is their primary role? A: Seraphim are celestial beings with six wings, primarily dedicated to praising and glorifying God (Isaiah 6:1-3).
2. Q: What is the significance of Cherubim in the Bible? A: Cherubim are often associated with guarding sacred spaces and objects, symbolising God's presence and guardianship.
3. Q: What is the role of angels in biblical narratives? A: Angels serve as intermediaries between God and humanity, delivering messages, providing guidance, and offering protection.
4. Q: Who is the "Prince of Demons" in the New Testament? A: The Pharisees accused Jesus of casting out demons by the power of "Beelzebul," often interpreted as a reference to the "Prince of Demons" (Matthew 12:24).
5. Q: In what way did angels play a role in the birth of Jesus? A: Angels announced the birth of Jesus to the shepherds, declaring "Glory to God in the highest" (Luke 2:8-14).

**Questions on Spiritual Warfare:**

1. Q: What is the whole armour of God, and why is it important in spiritual warfare? A: The whole armour of God is a metaphorical concept representing spiritual protection and readiness, essential for standing against spiritual forces (Ephesians 6:10-18).
2. Q: How did Jesus respond to Satan's temptations in the wilderness? A: Jesus responded to each temptation with Scripture, demonstrating the power of the Word of God in

spiritual warfare (Matthew 4:1-11).

3.  Q: What are some strategies for believers to fend off demonic oppression? A: Strategies include prayer, using the whole armour of God, and renewing one's mind through the Word of God.

4.  Q: How does spiritual discernment help believers in the unseen struggle? A: Spiritual discernment helps believers recognise spiritual influences and make godly choices (Hebrews 5:14).

5.  Q: What is the ultimate source of believers' strength in spiritual warfare? A: Believers draw strength from the Lord and His might (Ephesians 6:10).

## Questions on the Cosmic Battle:

1.  Q: How does the cosmic battle between angels and demons impact the physical world? A: The spiritual realm has a direct influence on the physical world, affecting events, decisions, and individuals.

2.  Q: In what ways can believers be a light in the darkness? A: Believers can be a light by living out their faith with love, kindness, and good deeds (Matthew 5:14).

3.  Q: What is the importance of keeping an eternal perspective in the spiritual war? A: An eternal perspective provides hope and endurance, reminding believers that temporary challenges are surpassed by eternal rewards.

4.  Q: How does the unseen struggle reflect the ongoing battle for souls? A: The unseen struggle directly impacts the salvation of souls, emphasising the stakes of the spiritual battle.

## Questions on the Armor of God:

1. Q: What is the purpose of the belt of truth in the whole armour of God? A: The belt of truth represents a commitment to honesty and integrity and is a foundational element of spiritual protection (Ephesians 6:14).
2. Q: How does the breastplate of righteousness protect believers in the spiritual battle? A: The breastplate of righteousness guards believers' hearts and moral standing, preventing them from succumbing to sin (Ephesians 6:14).
3. Q: What is the role of the shoes of the gospel of peace in the whole armour of God? A: The shoes of the gospel of peace enable believers to stand firm and share the message of salvation (Ephesians 6:15).
4. Q: How does the shield of faith help believers fend off the devil's attacks? A: The shield of faith is crucial for deflecting the devil's fiery darts of doubt and temptation (Ephesians 6:16).
5. Q: What is the significance of the helmet of salvation in spiritual warfare? A: The helmet of salvation guards believers' minds and assures them of their eternal security (Ephesians 6:17).
6. Q: How does the sword of the Spirit differ from other pieces of the armour of God? A: The sword of the Spirit is the Word of God, representing the offensive weapon for believers in spiritual warfare (Ephesians 6:17).

**Questions on Spiritual Discernment:**

1. Q: What is the role of spiritual discernment in recognising angelic and demonic influences? A: Spiritual discernment helps believers differentiate between divine and demonic sources of influence.
2. Q: How can believers cultivate spiritual discernment in their lives? A: Spiritual discernment can be nurtured through

prayer, studying the Word of God, and seeking the guidance of the Holy Spirit.

3.  Q: Why is spiritual discernment important for believers in the unseen struggle? A: Spiritual discernment empowers believers to make wise choices and avoid deception from demonic sources.

4.  Q: What are the key signs of demonic oppression, and how can believers discern them? A: Signs may include negative thought patterns, physical and emotional disturbances, and recurring sinful behaviours. Discernment comes through prayer and seeking godly counsel.

## Questions on Looking Ahead:

1.  Q: How can believers actively engage in the battle for souls? A: Believers can engage by sharing the gospel, making disciples, and leading others to Christ (Matthew 28:19-20).

2.  Q: What role does renewing the mind play in the believer's spiritual journey? A: Renewing the mind involves transforming one's thoughts and beliefs through the Word of God, aligning with His will (Romans 12:2).

3.  Q: How can believers overcome evil with good, and why is this important in the spiritual battle? A: Overcoming evil with good involves responding to adversity and conflict with love, kindness, and righteous actions, demonstrating the transformative power of Christ (Romans 12:21).

4.  Q: How can believers maintain an eternal perspective in the spiritual battle? A: Maintaining an eternal perspective involves focusing on the eternal rewards that await believers and understanding that earthly challenges are temporary (2 Corinthians 4:18).

# About the Author

Andrew Lamont-Turner is a theological scholar, author, and Bible teacher who has dedicated his life to pursuing theological knowledge and disseminating spiritual wisdom. With a profound understanding of the scriptures and a passion for teaching, Andrew has emerged as a leading voice in the field of theology. His extensive academic qualifications and love for God and his family have shaped him into a multifaceted individual committed to nurturing spiritual growth and intellectual exploration.

*Academic Journey*: Andrew's academic journey reflects his thirst for theological understanding. He holds a Bachelor of Theology, Bachelor of Theology (Honours), Master of Theology, and a Doctor of Philosophy in Theology. These qualifications represent years of rigorous study and a commitment to excellence in his field. Furthermore, Andrew's intellectual curiosity extends beyond theology, as he also possesses a Bachelor of Education (Honours) and several Postgraduate Certificates in various commercial fields. This interdisciplinary approach has enriched his perspective and broadened his ability to connect theological principles with everyday life.

*Teaching and Writing*: Andrew's knowledge of theology has been expressed through his teaching and writing endeavours. As an educator, he has inspired countless students through his engaging lectures and insights into the scriptures. His ability to distil complex theological concepts into accessible teachings has garnered him a reputation as an exceptional communicator.

In addition to his teaching, Andrew is a prolific author who has published several books and a comprehensive Bible study series. His books delve into various aspects of Christian theology, offering insights, practical guidance, and thought-provoking reflections. With meticulous research, clear exposition, and a genuine desire to bridge the gap between academic theology and everyday faith, Andrew's writings have touched the lives of many, nurturing their spiritual growth and deepening their understanding of God's Word.

*Pastoral Leadership*: Living his faith ensures Andrew takes his Pastoral Leadership very seriously. He is the Pastor of a community church in rural South Africa, where he ensures the flock entrusted to him by God is well-fed and looked after.

Read more at https://ncts.education/nctseminary/course/view.php?id=25.